PROJECT MANAGEMENT
Combining Technical
and Behavioral Approaches
for Effective Implementation

PROJECT MANAGEMENT
Combining Technical and Behavioral Approaches for Effective Implementation

ROBERT J. GRAHAM

Management and Behavioral Science Center
The Wharton School
University of Pennsylvania

VNR VAN NOSTRAND REINHOLD COMPANY
New York

Copyright © 1985 by Van Nostrand Reinhold Company Inc.

Library of Congress Catalog Card Number: 85–637
ISBN: 0–442–23018–4

Manufactured in the United States of America

Published by Van Nostrand Reinhold Company Inc.
135 West 50th Street
New York, New York 10020

Van Nostrand Reinhold Company Limited
Molly Millars Lane
Wokingham, Berkshire RG11 2PY, England

Van Nostrand Reinhold
480 Latrobe Street
Melbourne, Victoria 3000, Australia

Macmillan of Canada
Division of Gage Publishing Limited
164 Commander Boulevard
Agincourt, Ontario M1S 3C7, Canada

15   14   13   12   11   10   9   8   7   6   5   4   3   2   1

Library of Congress Cataloging in Publication Data

Graham, Robert J., 1946
  Project Management.

  Includes index.
  1. Industrial project management.   I. Title.
HD69.P75G68   1985   658.4′04   85–637
ISBN 0–442–23018–4

TO MY PARENTS,
JOHN AND MARY GRAHAM,
CO–PROJECT MANAGERS EXTRAORDINAIRE

Preface

*The Philosophers have only interpreted the world
in various ways:
the point however, is to change it.*

*Tombstone in
Highgate Cemetery,
London*

This book is about managing people, project management, and change, particularly change in management style for project managers. It is intended to be read by new or prospective project managers, many of whom have been mismanaged on previous projects. The book was written with the intent of helping project managers develop a management style that does not perpetuate the bad management they experienced in the past.

Most people who attain the project manager position will already have a particular management style, a habitual way that they view and respond to people and situations. Most likely, this style is not based on reasoned thinking about which style might be most effective for reaching the project manager's goals. It is also probably not based on studies of human behavior in organizations. In fact, it may not be a result of conscious thought or conscious choice. Individual management style is usually the result of some combination of personality, experience, and habit.

A book like this cannot pretend to attempt to change your personality. Nor can the book provide experience, although it is based on the experience of many people. What the book can provide is a framework through which you can reinterpret your own experiences and then perhaps change some of your habits. So as author, I will take the job of the philosopher and interpret the experiences of this world of project management in various ways. These interpretations may suggest changes in the way you manage your projects. However, it is up to you—the reader—to actually make the changes. That is the point of this book.

The overall philosophy of the book is that project management is mainly people management, and not just planning systems and control techniques. It is assumed that people are motivated to perform activities on projects only to the extent that the activities they are asked to perform serve their personal values. Project management will thus be successful only to the extent that it enhances personal value attainment. Many of the management style changes suggested are thus geared towards the idea of managing people by helping them attain personal value.

The book is organized to develop an overall project management process which is based on the philosophy of achievement of personal value. Each chapter examines a certain aspect of the process. Most of the chapters contain some fairly specific suggestions for techniques which may aid in the attainment of personal value. However, they are not just presented, they are argued. That is, the WHAT to do is based on a reasoned argument of WHY it should be done. This is meant to serve as example, since it is assumed that an understanding of WHY things need to be done is a basic element in managing people. That is, it is assumed that none of us like to be told what to do without understanding why we are doing it.

Teamwork in project management is another basic concept. It is, therefore, suggested that if the book is to be used as a guide for project managers, it also be read by all of the other members of the project team. This is seen to potentially have at least two benefits for your personal value. First, it helps to explain to team members why certain practices are being instituted. Second, it will help you to change your habits because others will be better able to reinforce the behavior changes that may be necessary. (Team reading may also help me to attain my personal values and sell more copies of the book.)

I wish to recognize and thank many people who helped me along the way from book conception to publication. Some of the earliest ideas for the book came from conversations with Joseph Seltzer when I was at La Salle College. My thinking was further shaped by many of the people at the Management and Behavioral Science Center, particularly Chuck Dwyer, Dennis Cohen, Tom Gilmore, and Larry Hirschhorn. Other colleagues such as Kate Freed and Phil Pidcock added their suggestions, and the book is better for their input. I also wish to thank Gene Woolsey, who taught me a lot about the application of management science techniques. Special thanks are due to the many project managers who participated in my seminars on project management. They showed me much of the "real world" of project management and convinced me that managing people was indeed more important than managing technical control systems.

Word processing duties were ably handled by our staff manager Roz Long and then by Debra Graves. They persisted through the numerous rewrites and corrections, and were assisted by Michelle Henry and Kent Tyler.

Finally, I wish to thank my family who endured many hours of my absence as I peered into the word processor. Without the patience of my wife, Jean, and my children, Amy and Kati, this book would not have been written.

ROBERT J. GRAHAM
Philadelphia, Pennsylvania

Contents

PROJECT MANAGEMENT
Combining Technical
and Behavioral Approaches
for Effective Implementation

1
Introduction to the Project Management Phenomenon

Could everything be done twice
everything would be done better.
German Proverb

This chapter introduces aspects of the craft of project management. The following are some key concepts discussed in this chapter.

A project is a set of resources temporarily assembled to reach a specific goal. Even though projects may span a long time period, a key difference between projects and programs is that a project is normally done one time only.

Project management is the process of planning, controlling, and managing people as a temporary team. The environment of project management does not have the stability normally associated with more permanent programs. Project management is thus unique in that many practices associated with the management of permanent programs may have to be modified for the management of projects.

Project management can be conceived of as part of a total learning system in an organization. Learning is a creative experience. Following a project management process should help stimulate creativity in project teams.

Project management is not for the faint of heart.

THE PROJECT MANAGEMENT PHENOMENON

A project is a set of people and other resources temporarily assembled to reach a specified objective, normally with a fixed budget and within a fixed time period. Projects are generally associated with products or procedures that are being done for the first time or with known procedures that are being altered. Some examples of projects are the construction or renovation of new buildings, the introduction of a new product, or the achievement of automobile downsizing.

Projects are often begun as organizational responses to changes in their external environment. Organizations do not exist in isolation. As open systems, they are greatly influenced by the properties of their transactional environment. The transactional environment is normally conceived of as being composed of other groups or organizations which are encountered during normal task performance. Examples of such groups are customers, government agencies, suppliers, and competitors. The degree to which an organization thrives often depends upon how well it adapts or "fits" into its transactional environment. Since projects are a prevalent form of adaptation to environmental changes, the success of an organization can well depend on its ability to manage projects.

Project management involves the planning and execution of the utilization of resources in order to achieve a specified objective. These functions of management are fairly routine in stable environments. However, project management usually takes place in new or rapidly changing environments. For example, automobile downsizing projects began when imported cars constituted only a small percentage of car sales. As the projects proceeded, the number and type of imports increased rapidly. This development caused changes in some of the original concepts of downsizing as these projects progressed. Thus, since projects are temporarily assemblages in changing environments, they are normally volatile entities which require special forms of management. These special forms are collected under the heading of project management.

Since rapid change seems to be inherent in the project management environment, some people have postulated the "first law" of project management as:

> Few projects have ever been completed on time, within budget, and with the same staff you started with. Yours will not be that much different.

Such a statement does not bode well for the project manager. However, a manager can begin to understand such a statement by examining the reasons for the unstable environment. After the environment is understood, a manager can begin to devise an overall strategy, along with a set of tactics, for dealing with the challenge of managing temporary project teams. This is seen as the major task of the project manager—devising an overall strategy, along with a set of tactics, which can be used to reach the specified objective in a particular environment.

The overall strategy suggested here involves managing people as well as managing systems. In this book, managing systems is considered to involve the technical details of planning and control. This comes under the heading of the technological approach to project management and is covered chiefly in Chapters 3 and 4. Managing people comes under the heading of the behavioral approach. This approach is covered in detail in Chapters 4, 5, and 6. Various tactics to implement the overall strategy are explained throughout the book.

However, before tactics and approaches, we need strategy. How is the project manager to approach the task of project management? What are the forces that make project management different from regular management? How is project management similar to program management? These questions should be considered during the development of an overall strategy. We begin our strategy formulation with an understanding of the organizational environment of project management.

ORGANIZATIONAL ENVIRONMENT OF A PROJECT

Donald Schon has written in *Beyond the Stable State* (1971) that our organizations are moving from a state of bureaucracy to a state of "adhocracy," that we are moving from the state of the well known, predictable, and orderly to a state of the less known, less predictable, and less orderly. The management form most associated with stability is the classic bureaucracy. The position taken here is that there is nothing particularly wrong with bureaucracies as forms of management. They work well and are efficient for production in placid environments where the same or very similar products are produced repeatedly. Such environments give rise to the functional form of management in which people are grouped into departments by functional specialty, such as finance or accounting.

The hallmarks of bureaucratic departmental management are:

1. *Repeatability.* The same or very similar processes are used repeatedly to produce the same or similar products. The processes and products may be improved incrementally, but there is little experimentation.
2. *Predictability.* The products and the processes with which to produce them are fairly well known in advance.
3. *Boundedness.* Each department has specific bounds for its part in the overall process. For example, the accounting department does only accounting and everyone agrees to this. People from the accounting department do not attempt to do marketing or production, or any function considered to belong in another department.

To support all of this repeatability, predictability, and boundedness, an organizational culture or set of norms for behavior and interaction is constructed. This culture is itself repeatable, predictable, and bounded. Any culture is both learned and shared. The people who share a bureaucratic culture learn their repeatable tasks, how to behave towards each other, what to expect from each other, and what each other's specific tasks are. They also figure out the true reward system in the organization and how to advance through the departmental structure. The organization supports this behavior with rewards for conformity.

The organizational forms and operating cultures that arise in an environment of adhocracy are somewhat different from the bureaucratic case. As a result of the turbulent nature of the environment, new products are rapidly emerging. For example, it has been stated that half of the products we will be using ten years from now are not on the market today. Inexpensive calculators, home computers, and video-cassette recorders are examples of products that did not really exist ten years ago. It is also felt that the ten-year figure will be diminishing in the future. Advances in technology and the forces of competition, both foreign and domestic, mean that the processes of production are also rapidly changing.

The response to this rapid change will be a movement towards adhocracy. The hallmarks of management in adhocracy are given as:

1. *Nonrepeatability.* New products dictate new processes and vice versa. There is an air of constant experimentation and learning because of the constant change.

2. *Nonpredictability.* The results of the experimentation are often not known in advance. Totally different products may be discovered by accident.
3. *Nonboundedness.* Departments may not exist in the classical form. The structure will be "loose" since people are called on to perform a variety of different tasks. Accounting may be just one of the many skills that most people have.

To support this adhocracy, a culture will be developed which is flexible and task oriented (Handy, 1980). Within this type of culture, people will possess many skills and move freely from task to task rather than stay in just one role. The people who share this type of culture will learn how to function in multidisciplinary teams that are drawn together for nonrepeatable tasks, for a specified period of time, and then disbanded. The true reward system will be for performance and flexibility. Models for the management of such situations should not be drawn from the old bureaucratic model of the repeatable, predictable, and bounded manager. The adhocracy situation calls for a flexible and task-oriented, as well as people-oriented, manager who is not bounded by strict departmental affiliations.

An organizational culture can be seen as a pervasive way of life in an organization. It is composed of a set of learned rules, norms, and beliefs about the way work should be organized, about what should be done and the way things should be done in a given organization. A culture is established to help people who share that culture to solve a given set of problems. For example, a bureaucratic culture is good for solving technical problems that do not change much over time. This was the case before the breakup of AT&T. The old problems that needed to be solved were mainly technical problems of getting the telephone system to work well, and AT&T evolved as a classic bureaucracy.

However, as the problems change, the organizational culture must also change in order to enable people to solve the new problems. In the case of AT&T, the new set of problems revolves about imaginative new uses for the telecommunications system in place. These problems require more of an ad hoc culture. A summary comparison of the bureaucratic role culture and the ad hoc task culture is given in Table 1-1.

The task culture seems to embody the set of norms and relationships that are most appropriate for project management. However, that

Table 1-1. Summary of Differences in Role vs. Task Cultures.

CATEGORY	ROLE CULTURE	TASK CULTURE
General ethos of management	Logic and rationality	Get the job done
Work norms	Job description important	Job stresses individual, sensitivity to people,
	Do job as described by procedures	and self-control over work
Source of power	Position power due to job title	Expert power due to job knowledge
Pro and con	Good for routine	Good for innovation
	Bad for innovation	Bad for routine
Chief problem	Change	Control

culture may not describe your organization the way it is now. For an organization to move in this direction, the key is in the project managers. Therefore, many of the suggestions contained in this book are aimed at managers who are attempting to move the organization towards a project management culture. The suggested change process is covered in Chapter 10.

UNIQUE ASPECTS OF PROJECT MANAGEMENT

Managing a project is not the same as managing a department. To begin, a project is, by definition, something new, something that has never been done exactly like this before. As a result, the end product is often not fully specified in advance. In addition, the total process for producing the not-fully-specified product is itself often not fully specified. As a result, the project manager lives in an environment of constant uncertainty.

Sometimes, a temporary team must be managed for the temporary project. The team members may not be accustomed to working with each other. In addition, they will normally have a variety of skills and backgrounds, and thus a variety of biases, work habits, values, definitions of what is important, etc. The project manager must deal with all of these diverse people in such a way that they are formed into an effective working team. This is no easy task even when the people all have the same background.

Projects normally cut across departmental boundaries and also may involve many new actors in the transactional environment. Success will require much cooperation from the actors involved. Gaining such cooperation is often not an easy task. Thus, the project manager must be skilled in obtaining cooperation from other people over whom he does not have direct control.

The project manager normally works under strict time deadlines. The manager must deliver the not-fully-specified product, produced by a not-fully-specified process, but on a specified date. There is constant pressure around schedules and the monitoring of progress towards the due date. This often becomes the overriding concern of the project manager, often to the detriment of the final product and to the members of the project team.

In the past, scheduling and control have been considered the key to successful project management. Network planning techniques such as Program Evaluation and Review Technique (PERT) and Critical Path Technique (CPM) were designed specifically for planning and control of projects. These techniques are indeed important project management tools and are covered in Chapters 4 and 5 of this book. However, in applying these techniques, little concern was given to the behavioral aspects of projects. This was partially due to the fact that much of project management arose from the need of the federal government to plan and control product deliveries from independent vendors on large projects. The government was not concerned with how the vendors managed their people.

For the project manager in an organization, scheduling and control are indeed important. However, studies indicate that good human relations skills are also related to success in projects (Baker et al., 1983). This seems the more difficult task for the project manager is often managing people in a temporary environment, forming a team out of diverse personalities, and obtaining cooperation from people over which he may not have direct control. So planning and control are important, but managing people is the key.

These aspects of project management are only half of the situation that has been termed the interface management problems of project management (Stuckenbruck, 1981). The first set of problems involves the people interface problems among members of the project team. The second set involves the organizational interfaces, which are the interactions between the project team members and the different functional areas of the organization. These can be most troublesome as they involve not only people, but also varied organizational goals, as well as conflicting managerial styles and aspirations. Misunderstanding and conflict can easily occur within such interfaces.

So the project manager must be part planner, part psychiatrist, and part masterful organizational politician. In addition, he or she is often deeply involved in the creation of a workable project culture. Such a position is not for the faint of heart.

This book is designed first to deal with the people interface problems and then to tackle the organizational interface problems. It is emphasized that many of the people problems can be alleviated with proper team building in the planning stage of the project. If we assume that good planning and team building exist, a different set of problems arises during the execution of the project. Many of these problems involve the organizational interface, particularly the interface between the project and the organizational control systems. An organizational design which addresses many of these problems is the matrix form of organization covered in Chapter 8.

PRODUCT-PROCESS-CULTURE

At this point, we can specify different types of projects based on three of the variables that have been discussed, namely, the product that is being produced, the processes used to produce it, and the strength of the project culture. It will be argued that different aspects of project management, as covered in the next section, will be more or less important, depending on the type of project being performed.

The first dimension of the project type is the product being produced. On some projects, a totally new product is produced, while on others, a similar end product has been produced before. An example here is the difference between producing the Lunar Exploration Module (LEM) and producing a new office building. Both can be considered projects, but the degree of end product knowledge is strikingly different. The first dimension will thus differentiate the end product as

PRODUCT   Old ◁———————————————▷ New

The second dimension of project type is the process that is being used to produce the product. In some cases the process will be fairly well known in advance, while in other cases the process will be based on learning while doing. If the end product is fairly well known, the process may also be fairly well known. Then again, some projects involve creating a new process for producing a known product. Thus the product-process dimensions form a matrix of project types as follows:

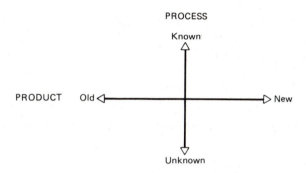

The final dimension of project type is the strength or weakness of the project culture. If projects are rare in an organization, then people may not be accustomed to working on temporary teams. The standards for interaction on multifunctional teams may not be well established. This would be called a weak project culture. On the other hand, the organization may have a tradition of using temporary teams. In this case, people will be accustomed to working on a multifunctional basis. This would indicate the presence of a strong project culture.

The project culture dimension can be used to split each of the four quadrants of the product-process chart. The final classification of project types is thus shown in Figure 1-1.

The argument here is that different types of projects require different amounts of emphasis on the different aspects of project management—namely, planning, control, and managing people. Generally, the less the product is known, the more emphasis needs to be placed on planning; the less the process is known, the more emphasis needs to be placed on control; the weaker the culture, the more emphasis needs to be placed on managing people.

From a project management standpoint, the simplest type of project would be one where the product is known, the process is known, and the culture is strong. However, this situation rarely arises in a project setting. On the other side of the coin, the most difficult project

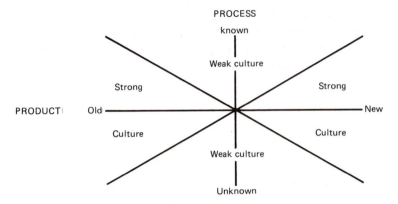

Figure 1–1. Product-Process-Culture Classification.

would be one where the product is unknown, the process is unknown, and the culture is weak. This would require much emphasis on all aspects of project management. Luckily, this situation also does not seem to arise often. Some point out that for the LEM project, both the product and the process were unknown. However, there was a strong culture. Everyone had "the right stuff."

With this guideline, we now turn to a consideration of the aspects of project management.

PLANNING-CONTROL-PEOPLE

Planning, control, and managing people are the three basic concepts of the project management process. Although they are listed separately, it is important to realize that they are interdependent. That is, the way you plan affects the way you control, and the way you plan and control affects the people on the team. In reciprocal fashion, the people on the team will often affect the way you plan and control.

Since each part affects every other part, it is the assumption in this book that all three parts should be considered together. This would mean that the people involved in the execution of the project should be involved in the initial planning and in the design of the control mechanisms. The three parts of the process are shown in the form of a triangle in Figure 1–2. It is important to note that all three parts are needed to form this figure and that all three parts interact in order to

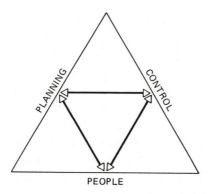

Figure 1–2. Planning—control—people.

hold it together. It is also important to note that people are seen as the foundation of this figure of project management.

Outline—Project Management Triangle

Planning   Planning is like life insurance. It is not thought of in a pleasant sense; everybody needs it, but it is not appreciated until there is a catastrophe. Project management planning seems no different. People often sense that precious project time is squandered planning when it could be used doing something constructive. However, the lessons from veteran project managers seem particularly clear on the notion that some form of planning is absolutely key for the success of project management. Thus, three chapters of this book are devoted strictly to the mechanisms of project planning. Chapter 2 motivates planning by outlining what can happen to projects without planning. Chapters 3 and 4 suggest the use of network planning and review some of the essentials for management.

Planning-   Projects do not normally proceed as planned. As the plan
People   is executed and more is learned about the true course of events, changes must often be made rapidly. Changing one part of a project can often have subtle but quite possibly disastrous effects on another part of the project.

The best changes are those made in light of the total needs of the project team. So it seems that the most important result of planning is not so much the final plan but rather the participation of the team members in the process of developing the plan. Such participation helps develop the team spirit and the total project comprehension that are so necessary for a successful project. Since managing people is key to managing projects, the rest of the book is devoted to various aspects of managing people in projects. Chapter 5 begins this emphasis by examining team building in projects.

Planning-
Control
The use of network planning techniques stresses the output of people in individual activities. Control systems compatible with this assumption should also stress results rather than specify behavior. This concept is called goal control. Chapter 6 explains some of the aspects of goal control and how it fits with project management. Techniques include the use of a work breakdown structure (WBS) and linear responsibility charting. Since most organizational control systems are activity oriented rather than result oriented, the organizational interface problems begin to become important at this point.

Control-
People
People will react to any control system to which they are subjected. Chapter 7 reviews the area of people-control management and covers such areas as perception, communication, and controlling the control system.

Planning-
Control-
People
The last three chapters tie together all three parts of the project management triangle. Chapter 8 reviews the matrix form of organization that some organizations have found useful for project management. Chapter 9 covers the essentials of creative management, a management philosophy designed to unlock and utilize people's creative potential. Chapter 10 discusses the problems of implementation of project management and creative management.

THE PROJECT OF PROJECT MANAGEMENT

Each organization is unique and each project is different. The people on any given project make that project unique compared to any other project, even if it is seen as the same type of project. A book like this can only give general guidelines based on the experiences of other people at another time and place. The experiences of other people in a different organization and organizational culture should not be assumed to be "the answer" to the project management problems in your organization. The general theories may be applicable, but the specifics probably are not.

To become truly proficient at project management, each organization needs to set up an organizational learning program. Such a program enables organizations to treat each project as an experiment and attempt to learn how project management works best with their problems, their procedures, and their people.

Organizational learning is a fairly new concept. According to Bedeian (1984, pp. 265–271), the concept rests on two fundamental foundations. The first of these is the notion of rational calculation. This concept incorporates the idea that organizations use expectations about future outcomes as a basis for selecting among current alternatives.

The second fundamental foundation is learning from experience. It is assumed that organizations adjust their activities based on past experiences in an effort to increase their competence. Thus experiential learning is typified by evaluation, assessment, and experimentation.

The basic characteristics of organizational learning are that it is a continuous process, that it embodies adaptive adjustment, and that there is selective attention to stimuli. The phases of organizational learning are cyclical in nature. This is illustrated in Figure 1–3.

The complete learning cycle assumes that organizations as a whole will act, observe the consequences of these actions, make inferences about the consequences of the actions, and draw implications for future actions. Despite the rationality and apparent importance of such a learning program, it should come as no surprise that complete learning cycles are the exception rather than the rule. It seems that examining the consequences of one's actions is just too painful or even dangerous in many organizational cultures.

Yet future action does take place. It seems that with both the com-

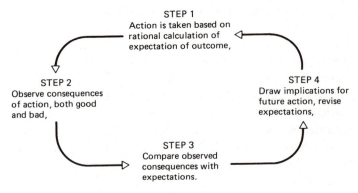

Figure 1-3. The organizational learning cycle.

plete and the incomplete learning cycle perspectives, organizations develop what Argyris and Schon (1978) have called *theories of action*. These theories represent beliefs that organizations hold regarding the consequences of their actions. With complete learning cycles, the theories of action are basically valid descriptions of reality. Incomplete learning cycles lead to theories of action with low validity. It would seem reasonable to assume that the more complete the cycle of learning, the more valid are the resultant theories of action.

Project management is action oriented so it would seem worthwhile to develop valid theories of action. The life cycles of projects make perfect vehicles for developing such theories. The project is planned based on some set of beliefs regarding the consequences of certain actions. The project manager can enhance learning by recording these assumptions at the beginning of the project. As the plan is executed, the people in the organization act. The project manager is in a position to observe the consequences of these actions. Individual learning will take place as the project manager realizes the difference between the predicted consequences and the actual results. Organizational learning takes place when these differences are discussed in an organizational context and become the basis for future theories of action.

A major implication of the preceding discussion is that a primary, but often overlooked, task of the project manager is the creation of a capacity for learning from the experiences of projects. Obviously, the creation of such a capacity requires sustained and detailed effort, effort which may not be rewarded in the short run. However, such effort is necessary in order to combat the tendency to continually recreate the wheel. The following suggestions are thus given on how to facilitate organizational learning:

1. An explicit commitment to educational ideals should be stated at the beginning of the project. This statement should be backed up by policies, procedures, and programs, together with an allocation of resources for such purposes.
2. Work experiences should be designed, as much as possible, so that team members at all levels can realistically expect to improve their knowledge and skills.
3. Recruitment policies should place an emphasis on capacities for learning, communication, and collaboration, as well as on the skills needed to complete the activities of the project.
4. A genuinely participative philosophy and practice should exist throughout the project such that individual members can, where appropriate, share what is being learned and enter into collaborative processes of decision making and problem solving on a regular basis.
5. An organizational learning and experiences paper should be scheduled and produced as part of the project's final report to management.

PROJECT PHASES AND PROCESSES

It has already been mentioned that management problems change over the life of the project. In Chapter 5, it will be argued that leadership style should also be changed over the life of the project. In this section, we develop a framework for understanding the reason for these changes by developing a general life cycle concept of project management.

The general life cycle concept is that projects have a beginning and an end, and go through several phases as they move from the starting point to the end point. The different phases have different characteristics, different sets of achievements and problems, and often demand different types of behavior on the part of both the team members and the project manager.

The number of phases in a project is an open question. Some say there are as few as three phases, while others feel there are as many as seven. Experience indicates, nevertheless, that however many phases there are, they often overlap, there is often backward movement to phases just completed, and few project managers can ever specify what phase they think they are in.

Despite the seeming lack of operational relevance of the life cycle concept, I believe it has conceptual relevance. The conceptual relevance is to drive home the place of the contingency management concept in the project management process. It seems that in the past, there was a search for the "one best way" to manage an enterprise. This search proved fruitless and gave rise to contingency theory. This theory basically states that there are several "best ways" to manage and the way to choose in a particular situation is contingent on the circumstances of that situation.

We posit here a four-phase model of the project life cycle, as illustrated in Figure 1-4. This is done in order to introduce some of the factors that influence management style. These factors will be further developed in the remainder of the book.

As Figure 1-4 illustrates, project phases are best conceived as overlapping. For example, after a project is created, planning may indicate that a part of the initial design is not feasible. This may cause the entire project to be rethought and parts of it recreated. Likewise, project execution may reveal flaws in the plan and signal a need for replanning. Most project managers are notoriously bad at ending, especially if that requires documentation, so it is often not clear when a project is indeed over.

Phase I—Creation

Phase I is the time when the project is first envisioned. Most of the members of the project team will usually not be present at this phase since it is normally done by top management. The potential project manager should be involved in this phase for two reasons. The first is that since projects are usually a reaction to something in the environment, there is often a sense of urgency surrounding them. The results

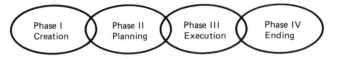

Figure 1-4. Four-phase project life cycle.

of the project were needed yesterday. This sense of urgency often results in top managers' dreaming unrealistic time deadlines for the results.

The second reason is that there is always a gap between what people visualize in their heads and what they explain to others. There are numerous examples of product failure due to the fact that the people who envisioned the product were not the ones who made the product. To avoid this problem, it seems imperative that the potential project manager be involved in all discussions of the potential project from the beginning. The management skills most necessary at this phase are creative thinking and interpersonal interaction.

Phase II—Planning

During the planning phase, the vision is translated into a project plan. The project manager must determine what skills are necessary and find the necessary staff. The project manager and the project team need to determine the necessary activities that will result in the specified end product. They must also determine schedules, responsibilities, and a control system. The chief management skill needed for this phase is team building.

Phase III—Execution

In the third phase, the project activities are actually carried out. The project manager is responsible for monitoring progress and for redesigning, rescheduling, and reallocating resources as required. The chief management skills necessary for this phase are delegating, conflict resolution, and shielding the team from the interference of well-meaning outsiders.

Phase IV—Ending

When the goal of the project is met, the project is terminated. At this point, the people on the project team must be reassigned. There is often much staff uncertainty at this time. Productivity often dips, and anxieties rise, as the end is near. The unifying force of the final goal no longer holds the team together once the goal is met.

Unfortunately, most of a project manager's energy seems to be directed towards completing the project rather than attending to the needs of the team members. Other project managers often begin to "raid" the team, looking for talent for their projects. Allowing this to happen gives the impression that the current project manager does not care how reassignments are made. This could be interpreted to mean that the project manager does not care about the team members' future. Spirer (1984) suggests that this is a very serious problem and that "each reassignment should be a conscious, deliberate choice." This will help the team members finish their time on the project with a better feeling. It will also help the project manager when recruiting for the next project, because it will have indicated that he or she cares about the future of the team members.

SUMMARY—THE COMPLETE PROJECT MANAGER

In summary, this chapter has reviewed many of the broad considerations thought to be necessary for successful project management. I thus posit the complete project manager as follows:

The complete project manager understands the transactional and organizational environments as well as the way in which the forces in these environments affect the project team. Such a project manager understands that most organizational policies aim to preserve stability while most projects aim to implement change. If the organizational culture tends towards the bureaucratic while the project culture tends towards a task orientation, this will be a source of constant friction between the organization and the team. The complete project manager understands that such organizational interfaces must be managed and not just left to chance.

In the area of project interface, the complete project manager is basically a team builder. In addition, this manager understands that projects must be managed differently depending on the newness of the product, the knowledge of the process, and the strength of the project culture. This difference in management involves engaging in various degrees of planning, controlling, and managing people.

The complete project manager is interested in the long term. As such, this manager will set up project management as a part of a learning system so that projects will be better managed in the future.

The complete project manager is flexible in management style. This manager understands that people need to be managed differently as the project progresses through different phases.

Finally, the complete project manager is a communicator. Much communication in organizations takes place almost automatically. When a new project is beginning, much of this communication is missing, mostly because the project manager and the members of the project team are new to each other. If the project manager is not a supreme communicator, he may inadvertently cause upset, as people begin to think he is attempting to benefit from what they believe is poor communication. To stress this point, I offer the first end-of-chapter reading, "Understanding the Benefits of Poor Communication" (Graham, 1981).

REFERENCES

Argyris, C. and Schon, D. *Organizational Learning: A Theory of Action Perspective*. Reading, Mass.: Addison Wesley, 1978.

Baker, B. N., Murphy, D. C., and Fisher, D. "Factors Affecting Project Success" in *Project Management Handbook* (D. Cleland and W. King, Eds.). New York: Van Nostrand Reinhold, 1983.

Bedeian, A. G. *Organizations: Theory and Analysis*. New York: The Dryden Press, 1984.

Graham, R. J. "Understanding the Benefits of Poor Communications," *Interfaces,* 11(3):80–82 (1981).

Handy, C. B. *Understanding Organizations*. Harmondsworth, England: Penguin Books Ltd., 1982.

Martin, D. M. and Miller, K. "Project Planning as the Primary Management Function," *Project Management Quarterly,* 31–38, March 1982.

Schon, D. *Beyond the Stable State*. New York: Norton, 1971.

Spirer, H. F. "A Systematic Approach to Project Termination," *Project Management Journal,* 73–83, September 1984.

Struckenbruck, L. C. "The Job of the Project Manager: Systems Integrator" in *The Implementation of Project Management: The Professional's Handbook* (L. Struckenbruck, Ed.). Reading, Mass.: Addison Wesley, 1981.

UNDERSTANDING THE BENEFITS OF POOR COMMUNICATIONS*

Robert J. Graham

There have been many reports of Management Science projects failing to be implemented even when it seemed that there were clearly obvious benefits to be realized upon such implementation. One such benefit that is often assumed during a Management Science project is that the development and implementation of a model will help to improve communications in an organization. This is particularly true with the normative type models such as PERT/CPM where improved communications is touted as one of the major benefits of the modelling process. Since better communication is often cited as a need in many organizations, one would think that models which aid in improving communications would be sought after with vigor. But experience has shown otherwise. This could lead one to surmise that better communication is not a desired goal in some organizations and that perhaps there are some people actually benefitting from poor communication. This essay will address the idea of the benefits of poor communication and argue that consideration of the effects of such benefits should be a part of any Management Science process.

The implementation of any decision aiding model can often be viewed as an innovation in an organization. With many innovations it is often true that the needs and wants of one group of people will be satisfied while those of another group will be frustrated. That is, one person's solution can often become another person's problem. From the literature on innovation theory (and from common sense) we know that the criterion of acceptability of an innovation is the conviction on the part of potential recipients that the innovation will, in sum, contribute more importantly to the satisfaction of a network of wants and needs than to their frustration. Based on anthropological studies of innovation failures, Anthony Wallace has concluded that:

> There now exists a sizable body of literature on applied anthropology, describing and analyzing situations wherein potential recipients refused to accept innovations that donors expected them to embrace warmly. The error of the donor generally lies in neglecting to assess the relevant negative functions of the proposed innovation: that is, incorrectly identifying the institutional motives that the innovation would actually tend to frustrate.
>
> [Wallace, 1970, p. 173]

I have seen and participated in this type of behavior many times. As Management Scientists attempting to "sell" a model we tend to emphasize those needs that will be satisfied and ignore (or not even think about) those needs that will be frustrated. A Management Scientist stressing the communications value of a model might find unexpected resistance from people who feel there are benefits to poor communication. It thus seems important that this phenomenon be well understood.

Kursch (1971) feels that when one calls for better communication at least four possibly erroneous assumptions are made. One assumption is that poor communication is mainly a problem of faulty technique. While this may be true in some cases, we will not address that problem here. The concern here will be with the cases where communication is poor despite the existence of good techniques.

A second assumption mentioned by Kursh is the assumption that better communication will reduce strife and conflict. However, it is often the case that better communication might tend to underscore conflicts rather than resolve them. Interdepartmental conflicts often exist in organizations and the process of combining two conflicting departments during the model building process could often serve to reopen old wounds and thus intensify the conflict. In addition, one department may feel that their turf is being invaded if a particular model is built, thus the communication that is usually recommended during the process of building a model could actually induce conflict rather than resolve it.

Another assumption concerning better communication is that when conflict continues for a long time, lack of communication must be one of the basic problems. But during any prolonged conflict there is usually plenty of communication but just not much agreement. In fact it seems that each time conflicting parties communicate, the net result is that each party comes away even more convinced of the righteousness of his original position.

The Management Scientist can often get caught in the middle of such a conflict. A manager might agree to a particular model-building effort under the guise of better communication but with the true intent of getting more ammunition for a particular conflict. If the results of the model add to the manager's store of ammunition, one could expect it to be warmly embraced. If not, one could expect it to be rejected. Note that in this case the acceptance or rejection of the model is independent of the correctness of the model itself. In addition it can be assumed in such a situation that if the results of the model do not please the one manager they would probably please the rival. The originally cooperative manager would probably not want such results known and would strive to keep them hidden—thereby adding to the poor communication cycle.

A final assumption often made when two parties are communicating is that it is in the interest of at least one of the parties, maybe both, to attain maximum clarity. In reality it is often in the interest of both parties to leave the situation fuzzy. To illustrate this point; I recently had the chance to quiz a group of executives on their perception of the benefits of leaving things fuzzy. I asked them to give their feelings about the benefits of poor communication. The results I received are listed below:

BENEFITS OF POOR COMMUNICATION

- Minimizes impact of poor planning (don't let others know you do not know what you are doing)
- Cuts down on questions, permits faster decision making, minimizes objections
- Easier to deny what you said later on; preserves freedom to change your mind
- Often a technique for gaining and/or maintaining power
- Good technique to mask your true intent
- Helps you preserve mystique and hide insecurities
- Allows you to say two things at one time
- Allows you to say no nicely
- Helps you avoid confrontation and anxiety
- Avoids the need to share credit for your ideas
- Encourages creativity; too much communication hampers thinking
- Helps minimize opposition and criticism.

From the list of benefits of poor communication it seems that executives feel that it is often to their advantage to leave things fuzzy. In fact, many executives fear the danger of clarity; making things perfectly clear can result in a loss of power and/or mystique. In addition, clarity has the disadvantage of tying the executives' hands and limiting flexibility in dealing with contingencies as they arise. Thus, even though an executive may be an honest and dedicated individual, he may not find it advisable to be too clear on future plans in order to avoid being trapped as situations change.

Some lessons for the Management Scientist seem clear at this point. The first is that if there is poor communication in an organization, there are a set of reasons for such a state. These reasons are usually not related to the lack of a model, management information system, or any other technical device. They are instead related to the motives of the managers; those needs, wants, and drives that cause people to act the way they do. As a model is probably not a part of the problem, it is also probably not a part of the solution. Thus it is important to first determine why communications are poor in the first place and work with the behavioral aspects of the problem before proposing or implementing a technical model.

The second lesson is that the Management Science process itself may induce conflict. It is often stated that all people who will be affected by a model should be involved in the construction of that model. This implies communication among departments. If one department is attempting to accrue the benefits of poor communication, you can expect that department to resist. If two or more departments are attempting to accrue said benefits, you can expect conflict to arise. The manager of the model-building effort should expect such conflict as a part of the Management Science process.

The final lesson relates back to Wallace's statement concerning needs satisfaction and frustration. With any change in organizational procedure the needs that are being satisfied or frustrated are often very subtle and usually not public. There are very few managers who will publicly come out against better communication. However, there are many who will resist initiative to improve communications. It should be clear by now that such is not irrational behavior but rather a manifestation of the difference between public and private values. It thus seems important for the Management Scientists to take into consideration the private needs of managers when they are attempting to determine if more needs are being served than are being frustrated.

References

Kursh, Charlotte Olmsted, 1971, "The Benefits of Poor Communication," *The Psychoanalytic Review* Vol. 58, No. 2.

Wallace, Anthony F. C., 1970, *Culture and Personality,* second edition, Random House, New York.

2
Projects Without
Project Management

Certain laws have not been written,
but they are more fixed than all the written laws.
Seneca the Elder, *Controversiae*
1st. Century A.D.

This chapter is a compendium of the experiences of many project managers working on many projects. It is an attempt to explain what some managers say are the inherent "laws" that seem to govern project planning and execution. The attempt to explain these natural tendencies of projects is made in order to devise management strategies to combat them. The project management process is based on alleviating some of the problems which will be discussed. The problems are introduced in the form of a saga of projects without project management. The main points of the saga are as follows:

Sufficient time is rarely allocated when the project is first formulated. The project manager must secure commitment to a tight time schedule.

Time schedules seem to slip in large chunks, when in fact they slip one day at a time. Network scheduling techniques could help monitor schedule progress.

When the schedule does slip, managers often seek a culprit. This is a nonlearning response. A better response may be for managers to seek reasons rather than culprits.

People from various departments start to accuse people from other departments of delaying the project. If this happens, the project team starts to lose cohesiveness as people defend themselves and their home departments.

When activities in the project are late, more people are often added to that activity. This response could delay the project even more.

When projects are late and team cohesiveness suffers, project results also suffer.

Network scheduling techniques represent a technical remedy for some of the scheduling problems identified. However, their use does not ensure a successful project. A combination of technical and behavioral responses will probably increase the chances of success.

A SAGA OF PROJECTS WITHOUT PROJECT MANAGEMENT

By definition, projects are large, unique, and complex tasks. The total project is composed of a set of interrelated activities. The project is not complete until all of the activities that compose the project are complete. The normal experience is that projects are not completed on time and within the original budget. One reason for this is the uncertainty in the project environment, reviewed in Chapter 1.

Another reason is what seems to be a natural tendency towards disorder in projects that lack proper project management. The typical saga of such projects seems to go something like this:

1. Sufficient assets are not allocated, and there is not enough time.
2. The schedule (if there is one) starts to slip, one day at a time.
3. The project manager suddenly realizes the slippage and seeks a culprit.
4. People from various departments involved accuse people from other departments of delaying the project. More time is wasted in finger pointing.
5. To make up time, the project manager decides to "crash" the project by applying more assets to all activities that are currently being performed.
6. Everyone scrambles to crash his job, and people are infuriated to find that they are either further behind or finished and their part is not yet needed. Interest wanes as people chafe under the new delays. The project is over budget due to all the crashing, and the whole thing is either

    a. on time but shoddy,
    b. well done but late,
    c. both shoddy and late, or
    d. abandoned.

Each of these elements of project failure will now be examined in detail as a basis for formulating a project management strategy.

1. Sufficient time is not allocated to the project.

One of the biggest headaches for project managers is often a simple lack of calendar time. It seems that there is never enough time allocated to finish the project. Some of the reasons for this problem fall under the general headings of external forces and internal optimism.

External Forces

The most important external force is normally considered to be competition. Many projects, particularly those concerned with new products, are instituted as a response to competition. When members of an organization learn of a competitor's new product, they often feel that they need a similar product very quickly in order to remain competitive. When this is the case, the completion date is often dictated by the competitor's product introduction date.

The case of competition is a specific example of a general problem, namely, that often the perception of the need for the project does not come early enough to allow sufficient time. Sometimes this results from a lack of environmental scanning, a lack of being aware of general developments in the business environment. In other cases, the changes occur too rapidly for a properly timed response. For example, gasoline prices rose rapidly in the early 1970s. This dictated a huge demand for smaller, more fuel efficient cars. Many of the makers of large automobiles did not have enough time to respond to the change and lost their market share to the makers of smaller automobiles. These corporations suffered as a result.

A second type of external force is financial. Often the need for a project is conceived in sufficient time, but the organization has insufficient financial resources to undertake the project. When financial resources are finally found, the amount of time for the project has diminished.

Other external forces include technological advances, government or regulatory changes, market changes in terms of demographics or sociocultural shifts, and changes in the supply chain.

Internal Forces

Probably the biggest internal force that prevents us from scheduling enough time is our own optimism. It seems that people brought up in Western cultures are prone to underestimate how much time it takes to accomplish their activities. This tendency often causes much anxiety. To add to our problems, we often become irritated when we fail to finish our activities by the date of our unrealistic estimation. When this happens, we generally reason that we did not work hard enough rather than realize that perhaps we just did not allocate enough time. The net result of such reasoning is that we often do not learn from our mistakes but continue to underestimate the time that is necessary. Such is the regenerative folly of time (under)estimating.

Another internal force that clouds our ability to schedule enough time is a reactive response to a superior's requests. When a superior asks if one can do a particular activity in five days, pressure is often applied or implied. The deadline may be unrealistic, but the worker will often commit to it with the hope of somehow completing the activity by that deadline.

An associated cause of the problem is failure to recognize the difference between actual time and elapsed time. Suppose that someone comes to you and asks you if you can complete a certain task in five days. You examine the specifications of the task and agree that you can do it in the time alloted. That person then leaves you with the task. He returns in five days to find that you have not yet completed it. How could this happen?

The answer might well be that although five days have elapsed, you have not been able to spend all of that time on the activity. During that time period there have been meetings, phone calls, and a myriad of other duties that are facts of organizational life. These other duties could easily take up half of your time. So although you estimated that the time it would take to complete the activity was five days of "real time," the elapsed time—that is, the number of working days between when you began the activity and when you can complete it—could easily be twice that. Thus it seems that the relationship between elapsed time and actual time is something like:

$$\text{Elapsed Time} = 2 \bullet \text{Actual Time}$$

When estimating the time to be alloted to a project, it is important to be certain to deal in elapsed time rather than actual time.

A final factor that influences time estimating is the experience of the personnel completing the activities. If a person is being asked to estimate how long it will take to do an activity he has done many times before, one can expect a fairly reliable time estimate. If a person is being asked to do an activity that is somewhat novel but also somewhat similar to previous assignments, one can expect lower reliability in time estimation. However, if a person is being asked to do something totally new, something that requires both learning and the development of new concepts, one can expect a fairly low reliability in time estimates. Thus it seems that the reliability of time estimates is directly related to experience with the activity. Since projects often contain novel activities, one should expect low estimating reliability.

Activity Completion vs. Time Expiration

Having dealt with internal and external factors that help cause an underestimation of time, we now examine one more aspect of time perception. This is the relationship between elapsed time and the percent of the activity completed. Figure 2-1 shows three possible relationships between the percent of time elapsed and the percent of the activity completed.

The first relationship is indicated by the straight line in Figure 2-1. In this case, the percent of the task completed is always exactly equal to the percent of time elapsed. Some people consider this to be the ideal situation, especially because it is easily accountable and easily managed. One knows immediately if one has fallen behind. However, such a relationship is usually only true for activities that have been repeated many times in the past. Activities that are new or different do not usually display such a relationship because of the learning and development that are necessary.

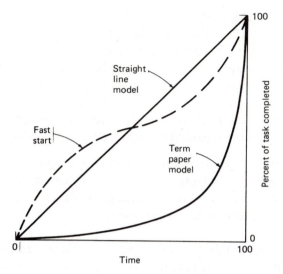

Figure 2-1. Some relationships between time elapsed and percent activity completed.

The two curved lines in Figure 2-1 represent various experiences with new or different activities. With one line, things get off to a flying start and then get bogged down. After some time, there is a resurgence of learning and the project races to completion. This is the "fast start" model. The second curved line represents the "term paper" model. This model seems to be associated with activities that require much learning and experimentation. With this model, there is little apparent achievement towards the final goal until about 80% of the alloted time has expired. After that, progress proceeds exponentially towards the deadline.

The "term paper" type of activity is probably the most difficult for a project manager. This is because the manager does not really know if the activity will be late until most of the alloted time has expired. Managing such activities requires a lot of self-confidence, along with a good measure of faith and trust that the required exponential increase in output will indeed occur.

Managing "term paper" type activities can add to the organizational interface problems mentioned in Chapter 1. The problem here from the project manager's point of view is that people outside the project may feel that there is not much happening, when indeed much learning and development are occurring. This perception by outsiders could cause a lot of friction with the rest of the organization. If projects are seen as essential to the survival of the organization, people will be concerned if it appears that nothing is being accomplished. There may be a call to change project managers or to otherwise interfere in the management of the project. Such interference is rare in programs but is standard fare in projects. The project manager is warned to beware of this "well-meaning" interference from outsiders.

2. The schedule (if there is one) starts to slip, one day at a time.

One of the best descriptions of this problem is given by Brooks (1975, p. 154) in his essay on "Hatching a Catastrophe." He explains the process of falling behind in this way.

When one hears of disastrous schedule slippages in a project, he imagines that a series of major calamities have befallen it. Usually, however, the disaster is due to termites, not tornadoes; and the schedule has slipped imperceptibly but inexorably. Indeed, major calamities are easier to handle; one responds with major force, radical reorganization, the invention of new approaches. The whole team rises to the occasion. But the day-to-day slippage is harder to recognize, harder to prevent, harder to make up. Yesterday a key man was sick, and a meeting couldn't be held. Today the machines are all down, because lightning struck the building's power transformer. Tomorrow the disk routines won't start testing because the first disk is a week late from the factory. Snow, jury duty, family problems, emergency meetings with customers, executive audits—the list goes on and on. Each one only postpones some activity by a half-day or a day. And the schedule slips, one day at a time.

Because of the inability to estimate time and the problems of time management already mentioned, we often begin with a fuzzy plan or set of milestones with little reflection on how the different activities affect one another. This type of behavior is often rationalized with the argument that since one cannot estimate or manage time, why bother? However, it is argued that even if times are fuzzy, the plan should not be allowed to be fuzzy also, as a clear plan helps group spirit.

It is important that the plan show the interdependencies of the dif-

ferent people on the project team. Such a plan will highlight the consequences of an activity being late, and it will indicate this in a very
personal manner because people will know who is in charge of each
activity. Personal knowledge of consequences helps build commitment to the team and the project. This commitment to others on the
project team becomes one of the chief motivating factors when the
schedule starts to slip. It brings out the extra hustle that gets the late
activity done on time. Network diagrams such as PERT and CPM are
excellent ways of indicating these relationships.

3. The project manager suddenly realizes the slippage and seeks a
   culprit.
   Attempting to find a culprit is a common reaction, but it is probably
not good management. It definitely does not set up a learning environment. However, standard project management encourages such
behavior on the part of the project manager. The project manager is
the person designated as the one responsible for delivering the end
product on time. When the schedule slips by a large amount, there is a
tendency to clamp down, tighten the controls, and show who is in
charge. While such behavior may feel good, it could destroy much of
the team building that may have previously been accomplished.

Schedule slippage is rarely the fault of one person. If there is any
one culprit, it is probably the project manager himself. However,
managers rarely find it advantageous to place the guilt on themselves.
Yet this is often exactly what needs to be done. The team members will
feel guilty enough and may be willing to assume some of the burden.
However, the project manager should be ready to assume the major
part of the responsibility.

4. People from various departments involved accuse people from
   other departments of delaying the project.
   When finger pointing occurs, the project becomes embroiled in the
standard organizational dynamics and loses some of its "special"
characteristics. Every organization embodies a history of tensions between various departments. The sets of attitudes that members of
groups hold towards each other can be the consequences of the nature
of their relationship or of some previous altercation. They can also be
due to a lack of understanding of, or empathy for, the functions performed by other departments.

In any case, a history of bad feelings brings out a set of defensive behavioral responses when a particular department is accused and thus attacked. An expected response is that people will begin to defend their home department. At this point, they take a position against the team. It is natural for people to defend their long-term position in a department at the expense of their short-term position on the project. This can be a killer to team morale.

Another problem to beware of is the case of the universal scapegoat. In many organizations, there exist certain departments that are traditionally accused of delaying progress. The personnel department often occupies this position, but it may be computer or operations or whatever other department is out of favor at the moment. The project manager is wise to prevent the project from falling into the organizational morass of blaming other departments for its own failures.

5. To make up time, the project manager decides to "crash" the project by applying more assets to all activities that are currently being performed.

When an activity is realized as being late, there is a tendency to attempt to speed up the activity by adding more manpower to it. One assumption behind this tendency is the concept of the man-month, the old idea that men and months are somehow interchangeable so that months can be bought by adding manpower. The oft cited example is that if it takes one person one day to dig a hole, and ten holes are desired, then the task can be accomplished either by one person taking ten days or by ten people taking one day.

It is not clear that this relationship ever did or ever will hold true. Such partitioning of men and months would work only where there is no learning necessary or no communication necessary among the workers. For some activities, these conditions may hold and the application of more effort could possibly affect the schedule positively. However, since special projects are normally learning situations, the activities of the project often require learning among the participants. By definition, learning among a group requires communication. In this situation, the application of more manpower could have a negative effect. Hence the man-month concept applied to special projects is thought to be a dangerous and deceptive myth.

To clarify the man-month problem, consider the following situation from Brooks' (1975, pp. 22–24) example of a software development project: Suppose a task is estimated for 12 man-months and assigned to three men for four months, with measurable mileposts at the end of each month. Now suppose the first milepost is not reached until two months have elapsed. What are the alternatives facing the manager?

1. Assume that the task must be done on time. Assume that only the first part of the task was misestimated. Then 9 man-months of effort remain, with only two months of calendar time, so 4.5 men will be needed. Add two men to the three assigned.
2. Assume that the task must be done on time. Assume that the whole estimate was uniformly low. Then 18 man-months of effort remain, and only two months of calendar time, so nine men will be needed. Add six men to the three assigned.
3. Reschedule. Allow enough time in the new schedule to ensure that the work can be done carefully and thoroughly, and that rescheduling will not have to be done again.
4. Trim the task. In practice, this tends to happen anyway once the team observes schedule slippage.

The first two responses could result in what Brooks calls a regenerative schedule disaster. Consider the first case as an example. Due to the learning that has taken place during the execution of the activity, the two new men cannot begin immediately. No matter how competent they are, they will require training and education by one of the team members. If this takes a month, then 3 man-months will have been devoted to work not in the original estimate. During the month of training, only two people will have been working on the activity. Therefore, 7 man-months remain from the revised estimate. This work needs to be done by five trained people in one month. So with the addition of personnel, the activity is now almost as late as it was one month ago.

In addition to training time, there is also repartitioning time to consider. The activity was originally partitioned for three people. Now it will have to be repartitioned for five people. This will add extra time for coordination and communication. Extra assembly time will also be needed when the parts are brought together at the end of the activity. This extra time could easily add 1 man-month to the estimated time. If this is true, then the activity is just as late after three months as it was after two, in spite of all the extra managerial and professional effort.

Note also that under the assumptions of case 1, even if we assume only training time, the second milestone will not have been reached by the end of the third month. When this is realized, the temptation is very strong to repeat the cycle and add yet more manpower. One can expect the results to be the same, namely, that the activity will be just as late again. The temptation will again be strong to add still more manpower. Therein lies the madness.

The regenerative schedule problem will also operate under response 2. So it seems that the only real solution is to reschedule. Most project managers do not like to do this, particularly if the activity is a critical one whose lateness will cause the entire project to be late.

There is, however, a possible solution procedure. Network planning techniques identify those activities that are critical or nearly critical. An activity is termed critical if lateness in that activity causes the entire project to be late. Normally, less than 20% of project activities are critical. If an activity is not critical, and the project manager is aware of this, then the activity can be rescheduled without affecting the entire project. This is true only if the reschedule is within the bounds of that activity's slack time (see Chapter 3, "Consideration of Slack").

If the activity is a critical activity, then the extra time can often be made up by scheduling extra assets for a subsequent critical activity that has not yet begun. This move will add to the subsequent activity's time due to partitioning, but since all of the extra manpower will be starting together, they will be learning together and training time will not be needed.

Network planning techniques identify all critical activities and their timing relationships. As has been argued, such knowledge is essential to the project manager once the schedule starts to slip, one day at a time.

6. Everyone scrambles to crash his activity.

People are infuriated to find out that they are either further behind or finished and their part is not yet needed. This causes interest to wane as people chafe under new delays. If the project manager has allowed the project to reach this state, it is doubtful that the project will be a success.

In some cases, this scenario is a result of poor workmanship and lack of knowledge. That is, the people who are on the project do not know how to perform the activities that are necessary. If this is the case, then project management will be of little help. As with most management techniques, it is assumed that people have the basic knowledge and skills necessary to perform the activities.

For most cases, however, it seems that the individual people on the project are competent but that the project itself suffers from inadequate organization and insufficient planning. Thus, despite the competency of each of the members, the total project team appears incompetent. Proper project management can alleviate many of the problems that cause such situations.

STRATEGIES FOR PROJECT MANAGEMENT

As stated in the beginning of this chapter, a saga was examined in order to gain some understanding of how things can go wrong on projects. This understanding can now be used to formulate strategies for better project management. There are two parts to the strategy suggested here. The first part is a technical approach and involves the use of network planning techniques. The second part is a behavioral approach and involves some behavior modification on the part of the project manager. The two parts are considered as a system such that both are needed in order to gain maximum benefit for project management. The two parts will be considered in more detail here.

Uses of Network Planning—The Technical Approach

Network planning techniques such as PERT and CPM are ideally suited to solve the planning problems given in the saga that has been presented. By breaking the project down into smaller components called activities and then plotting these activities in a graphical form, network planning techniques can be used to:

1. Determine the minimum amount of time that will be necessary to complete the project as it is originally formulated. This is done by calculating what is called the critical path through the network.

2. Show when the schedule is slipping by indicating the late finish time for each activity. The late finish time is the latest time each activity can finish without making the entire project late.
3. Show the interrelationships among activities so that members of each group can know which other groups are depending on their output. With this knowledge, various groups will know whom to notify when a delay occurs.
4. Indicate which activities are critical for the on-time completion of the project. An activity is critical if a delay in that activity delays the whole project. Likewise, if project time needs to be made up, it can only be done by speeding up the critical activities.

The use of network techniques addresses these problems only. One should not assume that the use of such techniques will insure that the project will be done on time. There is much uncertainty in the project environment that network techniques alone do not address, much less solve. One should expect unexpected delays because they will occur. Network techniques can, however, help you get off to a good start and perhaps minimize the effects of the (un)expected delays.

As an example of this idea, consider the results of research on some 650 projects by Baker et al. (1983). They state the following:

Is the use of PERT-CPM systems the most important factor contributing to project success?

No. PERT-CPM systems do contribute to project success . . . but the importance of PERT-CPM is far outweighed by a host of other factors including the use of project tools known as systems management concepts. . . . The overuse of PERT-CPM was found to hamper success. It was the *judicious* use which was associated with success. One military program was actually hampered by early reliance upon a network that covered four walls of a large conference room. The tool was too cumbersome and consumed too much time to maintain it. Fortunately, someone decided that the network was a classified document and ordered curtains to be placed over the walls. Once the curtains were up, they were never drawn again and the project proceeded as planned. More often than not, however, networking does contribute to better cost and schedule performance (but not necessarily to better technical performance).

So it should be clear that PERT-CPM is not all there is to project management. Networking is not a guarantee of success. It is best used as an initial aid to the team and not as a club in the hands of the project manager. Most of the benefit of networking is at the beginning, during the planning stages of the project. It is useful during execution to help find critical activities and show activity relationships. There are other techniques, such as work breakdown structure and responsibility charting, that are also useful during execution. It is the judicious use of both the technical and the behavioral approaches that seems to work best.

Review of the Saga—the Behavioral Approach

The project manager in our saga made some basic assumptions about people which caused some mistakes on his part from a behavioral viewpoint. In this section, we will review some of the possible errors and make some suggestions for corrective action. The very basic assumption underlying both the analysis and the suggested changes is that managers cause the behavior they observe and that this is based on the signals they send to their subordinates. More simply stated, you get back what you put out. The signals that a manager gives off are based in large part on his assumptions about people. This section thus begins with a review of assumptions about people.

Assumptions about People: Theory X and Theory Y

Douglas McGregor (1960) investigated the beliefs that people held about others in a work setting. He suggested that the assumptions that we hold about others impact on the way we behave towards them. In particular, he felt that many people who were managers seemed to have similar assumptions, which he called Theory X. These assumptions were that:

1. People are basically lazy and dislike work.
2. People are looking for security at work. They dislike responsibility, lack ambition, and prefer to be directed.

3. Because of Nos. 1 and 2, most people must be coerced, controlled, directed, and threatened with punishment in order for them to put forth effort to help meet the organization's goal.

McGregor noted that this set of assumptions was only one of several ways that a person could view others. He suggested an alternative which he called Theory Y:

1. Work can be as natural and enjoyable as play.
2. People like and will seek responsibility.
3. People can be self-directing and self-controlling if they are committed to organizational goals. Rewards can lead to this commitment.
4. Creativity and the ability to be a leader are widely distributed among the people in an organization.

The assumptions about people that a manager holds will tend to determine the behavior of the manager as well as the behavior of others who deal with him. For example, if a manager believes that his subordinates are lazy and do not want responsibility (Theory X assumptions), then he is likely to watch them very closely and tell them exactly what to do and how to do their jobs. He is not likely to give them much chance to make decisions. Over a period of time, his subordinates will learn to accept the situation and will not seek responsibility. This has been called a *self-fulfilling prophecy* in which the expectations of one person lead to the behavior in another person that meets the original expectations. If, on the other hand, the manager were to assume that people are self-directing, then a different self-fulfilling prophecy could be expected. In this case, the subordinates would be likely to use their greater self-control in a responsible manner and the manager would find that close supervision is not necessary.

One other way to view this is that Theory X and Theory Y represent the ends of a continuum. The manager needs to determine where his various subordinates are on that continuum and treat them accordingly.

McGregor (1960) also comments on the way many businesses are organized. He notes that people have learned to follow the Theory X assumptions because they are treated in that manner. As a result, much of the potential ability of the people in an organization is not fully utilized. Argyris (1957) has taken this argument even further and suggests that the modern organization is incompatible with mature behavior by its members (see Chapter 9 for a review of Argyris's argument).

Just as people have learned not to seek responsibility, if the conditions are right they can learn to seek opportunities to be self-directing. One of the basic conditions must be that they are treated as adults rather than as children. For a manager, this implies encouraging your subordinates to make decisions and take risks. In the beginning, a few subordinates may fail; however, failure is also a growth process, and helping others to learn has been argued as a task of the project manager. A good example of this type of manager is given in "MacGregor," an article by Carlisle (1978).

We have argued here that the way an individual sees his world will have an impact on his behavior. People with different beliefs about people and about the causes of their behavior will respond differently in situations because they perceive different solutions. In addition, expectations of the manager affect subordinates' behavior. If a manager expects to see hard-working employees (and communicates that), he is more likely to find that it is true because (1) there is a self-fulfilling prophecy and the workers' behavior is partially related to his expectation, and (2) he is more likely to perceive the behavior which indicates that they are hard working. Likewise, if a manager believes that his subordinates are honest, sincere, and self-managing, and he communicates this through his actions, he is likely to find that such is indeed the case. With this background on perceptions and expectations, we can now proceed with a behavioral analysis of the saga.

1. Sufficient time is rarely allocated.

The project manager may have acted as conduit for anxiety around time to be translated to the team. Whenever a manager focuses on one aspect of a project, the other aspects suffer. An early emphasis on time usually results in a short-term orientation.

Since the manager sets the example, his attendance to time and schedules will influence others to be anxious on the same theme. This takes the emphasis away from team members getting to know one another and beginning basic team formation.

Such behavior seems to be counterproductive since the solution to the time problem probably lies in the team itself. This solution is in team *synergy*. The concept of synergy is that team members can increase each others' effectiveness when they work together. The usual explanation is that the effect of synergy makes 1 + 1 equal 3. This can be very true in a learning situation. People usually learn best when they have the ability to interact with someone else who is also learning. In addition, it seems that the amount of understanding that two people can jointly have about a given matter is more than the sum of each individual's understanding. At the beginning of the project, the recommendation is for the project manager to stress synergy rather than schedules.

2. The schedule starts to slip, one day at a time.

One should expect the schedule to slip since a schedule is only an ideal. The question here is how the manager reacts to the slippage. If the manager attaches overriding importance to schedules, his reaction towards the project team members would probably be negative. If this is true, one can expect team members to keep the slippage a secret as long as possible while they try to catch up.

A more positive reaction is for the manager to seek out news on the slippage and use it for rescheduling rather than for berating project team members. With this approach, people will tend to volunteer information rather than keep it a secret.

3. The project manager suddenly realizes the slippage and seeks a culprit.

If this is the case it would seem that our project manager reacted negatively to information about slippage. If the realization came suddenly, then he got what he asked for (and perhaps what he deserved). As previously mentioned, the culprit here is quite clear—it is the project manager him/herself.

4. Members of the team accuse each other of delaying the project.

This is to be expected if the accusatory finger is pointed at team members. The project manager seems to have caused much of the problem himself, but he is not willing to take the blame. The team members know this, but they cannot or will not confront the manager about it. Probably none of the team members feel that they deserve the blame themselves, so they blame the only people left—each other.

This is the first step in team self-destruction. If the project manager does not intervene at this point, any synergy that existed will soon vanish.

5. The project manager crashes all steps to speed up the project.

As the team loses cohesion, negative synergy develops such that 1 + 1 now equals only 1. As the project slows down, pressure is put on the project manager to "do something." The typical response is not team building but rather to bring in fresh resources. This action could send a signal to the team members that the project manager lacks trust in them since he feels the need to bring in new people. As trust is an important ingredient in management, such a move could be demoralizing. Fresh resources should be brought in only after the team has been consulted and agrees.

6. Everyone scrambles to complete his tasks.

Here we enter into crisis management. The level of anger will probably increase and people will look forward to getting off the project. In addition, people may begin to feel that they do not want to work on another project with this project manager. The project manager may force behavior and be technically successful on this project. However, he may be setting himself up for future failure. Good people will no longer want to work on his projects. Thus for both short- and long-run success, it would seem that this manager could benefit from paying more attention to the behavioral aspects of project management.

SUMMARY

This chapter has raised many questions regarding the conduct of project management. The saga was used to illustrate and to attempt to explain some behavior commonly experienced on projects. Learning from these experiences, we posit these additional skills for the complete project manager:

The complete project manager understands various perceptions, reactions, and behaviors regarding time. He or she understands why people are normally optimistic regarding time estimates and adjusts schedules accordingly.

The complete project manager understands that the schedule will slip and that the personal commitment of team members is probably the best force that can be applied to catch up.

The complete project manager understands the myth of the man-month and is prepared to reschedule activities that fall behind and then to add assets to future critical activities as a way of keeping the entire project on schedule.

The complete project manager shields the team from well-meaning outsiders and guards that organizational dynamics do not interfere with team functioning.

The complete project manager uses a combination of technical and behavioral techniques to manage the project.

REFERENCES

Argyris, C. "The Individual and the Organization: Some Problems of Mutual Adjustment," *Administrative Science Quarterly,* 1–24, 1957.

Baker, B. N., Murphy, D. C., and Fisher, D. "Factors Affecting Project Success" in *Project Management Handbook,* (D. Cleland and W. King, Eds.). New York: Van Nostrand Reinhold, 1983.

Brooks, F. P., Jr. *The Mythical Man-month: Essays on Software Engineering.* Reading, Mass.: Addison Wesley, 1975.

Carlisle, A. E. "MacGregor," *Organizational Dynamics,* 50–62, 1978.

McGregor, D. *The Human Side of Enterprise.* New York: McGraw-Hill, 1960.

3
Network Planning Techniques

Men count up the faults of
those who keep them waiting.
French Proverb

Time is an important aspect in project management. This chapter deals with techniques that have been developed to help project managers determine how much time the project might take. In addition, these techniques help project managers determine where to put their management efforts in order to increase the chances that the project will be finished by the projected completion date.

The chapter is based on network planning techniques. A project is seen as a set of related activities, and network techniques are used to determine an initial schedule of those activities. Techniques for determining critical activities, constructing bar charts, and estimating activity time are also examined.

The chapter ends with a discussion of management uses of probability estimates of activity times in order to construct a triage system for allocating management time to activities.

INTRODUCTION TO NETWORK TECHNIQUES

This chapter is about network planning in project management. The basic concept of network planning is that a project can be seen as a set of interrelated activities. *Activities* are work units that must be completed in order to achieve the project goal. These activities and their interrelationships can be shown graphically in the form of a network. The network thus becomes a graphic representation of the work that must be done in order to complete the project. The graphic representation not only indicates time requirements but also shows dependency relationships among activities. That is, the network indicates which activities need to be completed before other activities can begin. With these relationships shown, the network becomes a central planning document as well as a central communication device for members of the project team.

To establish the network, it is most important to first establish the descriptions of the activities that need to be performed in order to complete the project. The next step is to establish the appropriate precedence relationships among the various activities. A *precedence relationship* between two or more activities is a statement of which of the activities must be completed before the other activities can be started. Determining procedence relationships is equivalent to determining which activities can be accomplished concurrently and which must be done sequentially.

If there is a precedence relationship between two activities, then the first activity is called the *predecessor* to the second, while the second activity is called the *successor* to the first. So if activity A must be completed before activity B can begin, then activity A is predecessor to B and activity B is successor to A.

A *project network* is a graphical representation of the relationships among the activities being done to complete the project. The network is assumed to begin with an activity and to end with an activity. The beginning activity has no predecessor activity, and the ending activity has no successor activity. All other activities in the network must have at least one predecessor and one successor activity. Any given activity may have more than one preceding or succeeding activity. However, no activity may begin until all of its predecessor activities have been completed.

A *path* through a network is defined as a sequence of activities that links the start of the network to the end of the network. Each path has a time associated with it. This *path time* is the sum of the times needed to complete all activities that are on the path. A given network will contain many such paths, each differing in the path time required to complete all activities. The *critical path* is that path through the network that takes the longest time to complete. This is called the critical path because it is the sequence of activities that determines the amount of time that the project should be scheduled to take. (Note that I say how long it is scheduled to take, not how long it will take.)

The activities on the critical path are critical because a delay in one of these activities will automatically affect the scheduled completion date. Noncritical activities are said to have slack time. This *slack time* is the amount of time that an activity can be delayed without affecting the completion date. Delay in an activity may cause a delay in the entire project if the activity delay is longer than the slack time associated with that activity. A critical activity is considered to have no slack.

NETWORK SCHEDULING EXAMPLE

The network concepts defined in the last section will now be illustrated using the following example. The data given in Table 3–1 show a project that has been broken down into ten activities. Each activity has been assigned an alpha character as a code for that activity. The second column of the table indicates the predecessors for each activity. Activity a is the starting activity and thus has no predecessor. Activity b cannot begin until activity a is finished. Thus activity a is listed as a predecessor of activity b. The final column lists the duration time expected for each activity.

The next step is to draw the network chart from the data given. Such a network chart is constructed from a sequence of connected lines, called *arrows,* and circles, called *nodes,* which represent the activities of the project. There are two main notation schemes used to construct the network diagrams. These are called (1) Activity on Arrow and (2) Activity on Node. Both of these notations are illustrated below.

Activity on Arrow (AoA)

With the AoA notation scheme, each activity is shown as an arrow between two event nodes, as illustrated:

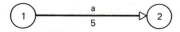

This is an AoA representation for activity a. With this notation, each activity begins and ends with an event. The beginning event for this activity is event 1, as shown in the left-hand node. The activity is represented above the arrow, and the expected time for that activity is

Table 3-1. Data for Network Example.

ACTIVITY	PREDECESSORS	TIME (DAYS)
a	—	5
b	a	6
c	b	10
d	b	4
e	c	5
f	d	9
g	e,f	10
h	g	5
i	g	6
j	h,i	5

shown below the arrow. The activity ends with event 2, as shown in the right-hand node.

The ending event for one activity is also the beginning event for the next activity. Thus the stream of activities a and b would be diagramed as:

Examining Table 3-1, we see that there are two activities that cannot begin until activity b is completed. These are activities c and d. When there are two or more activities with a dependency relationship on a single activity, then there will be two or more arrows emanating from the event that marks the end of that predecessor activity. This relationship, emanating from event 3, is:

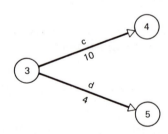

Likewise, when one activity is dependent on two or more activities before it can begin, then two or more arrows will be headed into the event which marks the beginning of that dependent activity. Examining Table 3-1, we see that activity g is dependent on activities e and f. Thus the arrows representing activities e and f would both be leading to the event that marks the beginning of activity g. This is represented as

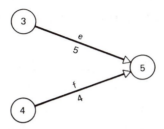

This graphical procedure continues as illustrated until the final event of the final activity. At that point, the network diagram is complete. The complete AoA network diagram for the example problem is given in Figure 3-1.

Most of the early project planning techniques utilized the AoA notation. After some experience with this notation, a new notation was developed which is now called the Activity on Node (AoN) notation. AoN notation is said to be less cumbersome than AoA notation. This may be true. However, it seems that the notation used is more a matter of personal preference than of proven ease or clarity. My personal preference is for AoN notation. Therefore, this notation will now be illustrated and used for the rest of the book.

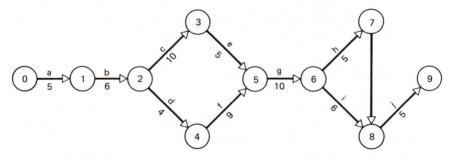

Figure 3-1. Sample problem—activity on arrow notation.

Sample Problem—Activity on Node (AoN)

With AoN notation, the construct of the event is not used. Activities are represented in the node itself, and the arrow is used to represent movement from a predecessor activity to a successor activity. The alpha code for the activity and the expected time duration for that activity are usually both placed inside the node. Thus, the relationship of activities a and b would be shown as follows with AoN:

An activity which has two or more successor activities depending on it will be shown with two or more arrows emanating from the node representing it. Likewise, an activity which depends on two or more other activities before it can begin will have two or more arrows leading into the node that represents it. Thus, the relationship among activities b,c,d,e, and f would be charted as follows:

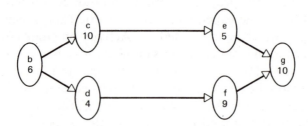

The complete AoN network for the example problem is shown in Figure 3–2. Included on this diagram are numbers for early and late start and finish times which will be derived in subsequent sections.

THE CONCEPT OF THE CRITICAL PATH

At this point, we examine Figure 3–2 and consider the concept of paths through the network. A path is any consecutive string of activities that leads from the first activity to the last activity. A path is an artificial construct useful for examining networks. It does not repre-

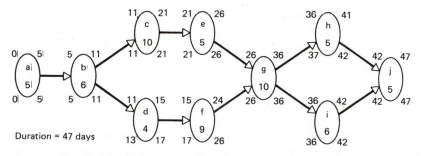

Figure 3-2. Sample Problem—Activity on node notation.

sent the way in which the project will be completed. All activities must be completed before the entire project is completed. A project cannot be completed merely by completing the activities along one particular path.

From Figure 3-2 we see that there are four paths through the network. Each path has an associated path time, which is the sum of the activity times of all activities on the path. The four paths and their total times are given in Table 3-2. The *critical path* is defined as the path with the longest total time. This longest total time is the minimum amount of time in which the project can be completed. In this example, the minimum amount of time for the entire project is 47 days. This is associated with path 3, which is thus the critical path.

All of the activities on the critical path are considered to be critical activities. This is due to the fact that any delay in those activities will automatically delay the entire project, unless the time can be made up in subsequent activities. In the example of Figure 3-2, there are only three activities that are not critical. These are activities d,f, and h. Looking at activity h, we can see that this activity can be delayed by one day without delaying the entire project. This is due to the fact that activity h is being done at the same time as activity i. Since activity i

Table 3-2. Network Path Times.

NETWORK PATHS	TOTAL TIME (DAYS)
1. a-b-c-e-g-h-j	46
2. a-b-d-f-g-h-j	44
3. a-b-c-e-g-i-j	47
4. a-b-d-f-g-i-j	45

will take six days and since activity j cannot begin until after that sixth day, then activity h can delay for 1 day without affecting the start of activity j. This one "extra" day for activity h is called the *slack* time for that activity.

CALCULATING THE CRITICAL PATH

For most networks, the critical path is not as obvious as in the sample problem. Usually the critical path is determined by using numerical techniques, often with the aid of a computer. The numerical techniques also yield slack times available for each activity. Such a technique is now illustrated using the example problem (Figure 3–2).

To calculate the critical path, the following numbers need to be determined for each activity:

Early start time—this is the earliest time that the activity can begin. If the activity times are in days, then this is the earliest day that the activity can begin. By convention, the early start time for the first activity in a network is considered as day zero.

Early finish time—this is the earliest time that the activity can finish. The early finish time for any activity becomes the early start time for any subsequent activities for which it is a predecessor.

Late start time—this is the latest time that the activity can begin without delaying the entire project. For activities on the critical path, the late start time is the same as the early start time. For non-critical activities, the late start time will be later than the early start time, and the difference between the two will define the amount of slack for that activity.

Late finish time—This is the latest time that the activity can finish without affecting the scheduled completion date. For activities on the critical path, the late finish time will be the same as the early finish time.

The notation used here is to place the numbers for the various times around the nodes representing the various activities. The early start (ES) time is placed to the upper left of the node, and the early finish (EF) is placed to the upper right portion. Likewise, the late start (LS) time is placed to the lower left portion, and the late finish (LF) time is placed to the lower right portion. Thus the notation on each node looks as follows:

Calculations proceed in the following manner:

1. Place the starting time value on the upper left portion of the first activity node. This is usually given as a zero, but it may be a calendar date or a start time in the future. This is the early start time of this activity.
2. Add to the starting time the activity time contained in the node, and place this number to the upper right of the node. This is the early finish time of this activity.
3. Examine the next unmarked activity, all of whose predecessors have been marked with ES and EF times. Mark above and to the left of this activity the largest EF time of any of its immediate predecessors. This becomes the ES time for this activity.
4. Calculate the early finish time as EF = ES + activity time, and place that number above and to the right of the activity node.
5. Repeat steps 3 and 4 until the last activity has been marked. The early finish time for the entire project will be the EF time for the last activity.
6. The critical path is determined by following the largest early finish numbers while working backwards through the network from the last activity to the first.
7. Now determine the late finish time for the entire project, and place that number below and to the right of the final activity. The late finish time can be taken as the early finish time if the project is to have no slack along the critical path.
8. Subtract the activity time from the LF time to arrive at the late start time, and place this number below and to the left of the node.

9. Working backwards, consider any new activities which are unmarked with LS and LF times. Mark below and to the right of the node the smallest LS time marked on any of its immediate successors.
10. Repeat steps 8 and 9 until all activities have been completely marked. The LS number of the first activity is the latest time that the entire project can be started and still have the project finish on time (if one assumes no resource reallocation on the critical activities).

Following these calculation steps, one arrives at the completely marked network diagram, as shown in Figure 3–2. The reader is encouraged to work through the sample problem at this point and then check his answers with those given in Figure 3–2.

Constructing network charts represents the first step in constructing a project plan. It should be evident that network diagrams are very good for indicating activity relationships. Using this diagram, each person on the project team will know exactly who (or least which activity) is depending on the output of his activity and when it is expected. If an activity falls behind, each person should know who will be the most immediately affected by the slippage.

Network diagrams are also good for determining the critical path, the critical activities, and the amount of slack in noncritical activities. This information is extremely useful to the project manager. When a project begins to fall behind, it is those future critical activities that hold the key to making up the time. Since projects appear to be prone to falling behind, it would seem to be critically important for the effective project manager to know the critical activities before the project begins.

CONSTRUCTING BAR CHARTS

While network diagrams are fairly good at representing activity relationships and critical paths, they do not usually do well at representing project time duration or the relative time of various activities. The usual solution to this problem is to construct a bar chart to be used along with the network chart. A bar chart for the problem given in Figure 3–2 is shown in Figure 3–3.

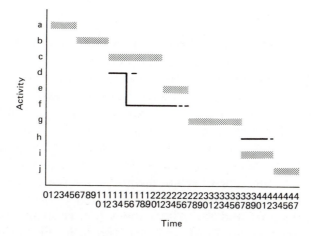

Figure 3-3. Bar chart for sample problem in Figure 3-2.

As indicated in Figure 3-3, a bar chart is constructed by listing the activities on the vertical axis and a time line on the horizontal axis of a graph. The time length of each activity is then indicated by the length of the line drawn next to the activity code. By using different symbols, additional bits of information can also be coded on the chart. For the example given in this figure, critical activities are shown by a double lines (=), noncritical activities are shown by a single line (−), and the activity slack is shown by dots (.).

Activity relationships can also be seen on a bar chart, although with a bit more difficulty. The relationship between critical activities can be found by looking at the end of a given critical activity and then looking down on the chart to see where the next critical activity begins. Relationships between noncritical activities are not as easy to see. For example, in Figure 3-3, we know that activities d and f are related such that using two days of slack on activity d will eliminate that much slack for activity f. This relationship can be shown by the vertical line connecting the end of activity d with the beginning of activity f. Using slack time can be thought of as moving activity d to the right two spaces. The vertical line can be thought of as a connecting rod such that if activity d moves to the right by two spaces, activity f will also move right two spaces. With activity f moved to the right two spaces, there is no longer any slack left for that activity. With this device, the connection between the two activities becomes much clearer.

CONSIDERATION OF SLACK

The concept of activity slack becomes very important when it comes to actually scheduling activities not on the critical path or when it is necesary to reallocate assets from noncritical to critical activities. Since activities with slack are often connected to other activities, using the slack on one activity will affect the connected avtivity. This has been illustrated with the example of activities d and f in Figure 3–3. This case shows that activity slacks can be related in such a way that one adtivity's slack can be used up when a predecessor activity fails behind.

To designate this type of relationship, we use the concepts of total slack and free slack. The *total slack* of an activity is the difference between its late start and early start times (or, equivalently, the difference between its late finish and early finish times). In the example of Figure 3–2, activities d and f both have a total slack of two days while activity h has a total slack of one day.

Given the possibilities of relationships between activities with slack, we also use the concept of free slack. *Free slack* is the amount of time a job can be delayed without affecting the early start time of any other job. The free slack for any activity can be calculated as the difference between its early finish time and the earliest of the early start times of all of its immediate successors. Thus in the example of Figure 3–2, activity d has zero free slack. However, activity f has two days of free slack and activity h has one day of free slack. This is an indication that using the slack of activity d will affect the start time of a subsequent activity, but using the slack of activity f or h will not affect the start time of any subsequent activities. Knowledge of this is important lest the project manager think that there are a total of four days of slack when activities d and f are considered. It is important to know both the total slack and the free slack for each activity.

Once activity networks have been drawn, further calculations can be made using either PERT (Program Evaluation and Review Technique) or CPM (Critical Path Method). We turn now to a consideration of those techniques.

THE PERT MODEL

Both PERT and CPM use network diagrams as a starting point. In addition, the notions of critical path and activity slack are common to both techniques. The difference between the two techniques is a matter of emphasis. With PERT, the emphasis is on estimating time, and the model incorporates concepts from probability in order to get the best possible estimates. Cost is considered to be associated with time, but it is not considered explicitly. With CPM, the emphasis is on time and cost trade-offs. The time to complete an activity is assumed to be known, and it is further assumed that this time can be reduced, down to a known limit, with corresponding increases in cost.

The PERT model seems to find most application in situations in which the products and processes are not well known but the culture is fairly strong—for example, research and development programs. CPM, on the other hand, has most frequently been applied to construction-type projects where the products and processes are fairly well known but the personnel and location are different, and thus there is not a strong culture.

PERT assumes that the network relationships have been well defined but that there is little past history on which to base the time estimates. Rather than base all calculations on a single number (most likely a guess), the PERT model requires time estimators to think in terms of ranges. That is, the time estimator is asked to think in terms of a range of time that it would take to complete an activity and to specify a minimum, a maximum, and a most likely time for each activity. Thus the PERT model requires not one but three time estimates for each activity. These are defined as:

a   the *optimistic* estimate. This is the shortest conceivable time for the activity. This estimate assumes that everything will go right and there will be no delays.

b   the *pessimistic* estimate. This is the best guess for the maximum time it would take to complete an activity if bad luck were encountered at every turn. This estimate does not allow for catastrophies such as earthquakes, floods, or nuclear war. It is to reflect delays that could be expected during the normal work process.

m   the *most likely* time. This is the best guess of the time the activity will take if the estimator assumes the normal number of foul-ups and lucky breaks that have been encountered in the past. This should not be considered as the average of *a* and *b*.

Expected Activity Time

Given the estimates just described, the next step is to combine them to arrive at a single number called the expected activity time. The combining formula rests on the assumption that the optimistic and pessimistic activity times are about equally likely to occur. There is also an assumption that the most likely time is four times more likely to occur than either of the other two. If one applies these assumed weights to the three time estimates, the formula for calculating the expected activity time, t, becomes:

$$ t = \frac{a + 4m + b}{6} $$

We should pause for a moment to consider the concept of expected time. This is a concept from probability used to designate the average time that would be expected if the activity were repeated often. It is a confusing term because often the expected time is not expected on any single repetition of an activity.

To illustrate this, suppose an activity is designated as flipping a coin. On each repetition of this activity, the coin flipper is to get $1.00 for a head and $0 for a tail. If one assumes a fair coin where heads and tails are equally likely, the expected return for each flip is $.50; half of the time it will be $1.00, and half of the time it will be $0. However, on any given flip, the coin flipper does not expect $.50—he expects either one dollar or nothing. This illustrates the semantic problem involved in using probability concepts. Some people become upset because the expected time is never expected.

The key here is not to confuse the expected time with the most likely time. The most likely time is what is expected for this one time that the activity will be done, if the normal number of foul-ups are assumed. The expected activity time is the result of a mathematical formula.

Thus, suppose that for activity a from the example, the person who was going to perform that activity gave us three estimates:

a—most optimistic $= 2$
b—most pessimistic $= 20$
m—most likely $= 5$

Using the formula, we would calculate the expected activity time as:

$$t = \frac{a + 4m + b}{6} = \frac{2 + (4)(5) + 20}{6} = 7$$

Here the expected time is larger than the most likely time. This results from the relatively large number given for the most pessimistic time. Additional estimates and expected times for the sample problem (Figure 3–2) are given in Table 3–3.

Variability of Activity Times

Using three time estimates to calculate expected activity times adds another dimension to our thinking about projects. This dimension is thinking of completion times in terms of ranges of days instead of just one particular day. This concept will be applied to the entire project in the next section. Before doing that, however, we must first explore the concept of variance of activity times.

The key to the concept of *variance* is the idea of variability and trust. Looking back on the data in Table 3–3, we see two activities, b and i, for which the expected time is 6 and the most likely time is 6. The question on variability becomes, Which one of the estimates do you trust the most? Most people feel that activity i is more likely actually to be done in six days because the optimistic and pessimistic times are so

Table 3–3. Time Estimates for Sample Problem (Figure 3–2).

ACTIVITY	OPTIMISTIC	PESSIMISTIC	MOST LIKELY	EXPECTED TIME
a	2	20	5	7
b	2	10	6	6
c	3	11	10	9
d	3	11	4	5
e	2	14	5	6
f	8	22	9	11
g	3	17	10	10
h	2	26	5	8
i	5	7	6	6
j	2	20	5	7

close to the most likely time. In this case, we say that the estimate does not vary much. Thus, this activity has low variability.

The estimates of the most likely time for activity b in Table 3–3 vary much more widely. This wide range of estimates represents greater uncertainty and, hence, less confidence in our ability to anticipate correctly the actual time that the activity will require. Thus our measure of variability is inversely related to the reliability of our estimates. That is, the higher the variability, the lower is our confidence that the activity will be completed by the expected activity time.

One measure of variability of activity times is given by the variance, a commonly used statistical measure of variability among numbers. The *variance* is the average squared difference of all numbers in a set from the mean of those numbers. An associated statistic is the *standard deviation,* which is the square root of the variance.

For the PERT process, the calculation of the standard deviation, *s,* has been greatly simplified. The formula for the standard deviation for any expected activity time is given as:

$$s = \frac{b - a}{6}$$

Using the data given in Table 3–3, we see that the standard deviation for activity b is:

$$s = \frac{b - a}{6} = \frac{10 - 2}{6} = 1.33$$

Likewise, the standard deviation of activity i can be calculated to equal 0.33.

By themselves, these numbers do not mean much. They are used mainly for comparison purposes. Since the standard deviation is directly related to the variance, the relationship between the standard deviation and the reliability is the same as the relationship between the variance and the reliability. Thus a higher standard deviation represents a higher degree of uncertainty regarding expected activity time. With a higher standard deviation, there is a greater chance that the actual time required to complete an activity will differ significantly from the expected activity time.

Expected Project Time

The concepts associated with expectation and variance of activity times can be expanded to the total project time. Since PERT works with ranges of each activity, it also works with ranges for the entire project. We will reconsider the sample problem of Figure 3-2 using the data from Table 3-3.

The critical path calculations for expected project time employ the expected activity time figures for each activity. Using these figures, we see that the critical path has changed from our first calculations, shown in Table 3-2. The new critical path is given as a-b-d-f-g-h-j. The sum of the expected activity times, the expected project time, is now 54 days.

Similarly, the variance of a sum of independent activity times is equal to the sum of their individual variances. Thus the variance of the expected project time is the sum of the variances of those activities that are on the critical path. Using the data from Table 3-1, we see that the variance of the expected project time is 3.46 and that the standard deviation is therefore 1.86. Remember that these numbers mean very little by themselves. They are used as an indication of reliability. The higher the standard deviation of the expected project time, the more likely it is that the actual time required to complete the project will differ from the expected time.

Having calculated the variance of the expected project time, one can now calculate the probability that the project will be done by a certain day. To do this, however, one needs to make giant leaps of faith regarding the use of probability concepts to describe unique events. The leaps of faith required are discussed in the next section. Those desiring to make these leaps and to actually calculate the probabilities, are referred to Wiest and Levy (1977, pp. 48–52) for details on the procedure.

USING PROBABILITY IN PROJECT MANAGEMENT

There are pros and cons of using probability concepts for unique events such as projects. The pros are in the area of sensitizing the project manager to the concepts of ranges and probabilities. The cons are that the concepts of probability do not really fit well with unique events. The entire idea of probability is built on repeatable events. Applying the concepts incorrectly can give false impressions. Perhaps this is best explained by the following example.

Assume that you are one of three U.S. citizens who are touring the Banana Republic and are thrown in jail. The Generalissimo has decided that to celebrate the anniversary of the glorious revolution, which is tomorrow, he is going to shoot an American tourist as a symbol of his feelings towards the United States. He is totally indifferent about which one of the three tourists he will shoot. As you sit in your cell, you ponder the probability that you will be shot tomorrow. What is it?

Many people reason that since there are three people in the cell and the Generalissimo is indifferent as to which of you will be shot, this represents a random draw of one from a population of three and thus your probability is 1/3. This would be the answer from classical statistics.

However, another view is that this is not a repeated event but rather a one-shot deal (so to speak). As you look across the cell, you know with certainty that one of the people there will not be shot tomorrow, although you do not know which one. So in reality, the choice lies between you and one other person. In that case, your probability is 1/2.

Now arguing whether the real probability is 1/2 or 1/3 is probably not very productive. By tomorrow you will be either shot or not shot, and so the whole question will become moot. At least today, you can think in terms of general ranges of probabilities and take some solace in the fact that your probability is not 90%.

The same is true for project managers. Calculating variances gives some general indications, but the numbers should not be taken literally. Perhaps the more important result of these calculations is the realization that the critical path has a variance and the other paths also have variances. Some project managers have stated that the path that is really critical is the one with the highest variance.

It may be true that under some combination of activity times and variances, a near-critical or "shadow" critical path may exist with higher variance than the "official" critical path. If bad luck is experienced along this path, it could easily turn out to be longer than the original critical path. Thus where the possibility of variance in activity times is admitted, the possibility of alternate critical paths is implied. Wags suggest that it is usually the near-critical path that turns out to cause the problems. Thus it is generally felt that the simple estimation of one critical path tends to yield overly optimistic results.

LEVELS OF ACTIVITY MANAGEMENT

The information from network charts, bar charts, and the PERT process yields both planning and operational guidance. With the introduction of the idea of the near-critical path, a three-tier framework of activities arises, a sort of triage scheme for management attention to activities. The three levels are defined here:

Level 1—These are the activities that require maximum management attention during both planning and execution of the project. Activities on the critical path are the level 1 activities. Activities on any near-critical path can also be level 1 activities, especially if the variance of those activities is high. If the variance on any near-critical path is higher than the variance of the "real" critical path, then all activities on the near-critical path should be considered in level 1.

Level 2—These activities require less management attention. Included in the category would be any near-critical path activities that are not in level 1 and any other activities that have high variance. In addition, activities with zero free slack should also be placed in this category because delay in these activities will affect at least one subsequent activity, although it may not affect the project as a whole.

Level 3—These activities require very little management attention. They are activities with medium or low variance and some amount of free slack. If these activities fall behind, there is usually little urgency.

The project manager's time is probably the scarcest resource on the project. This classification can be used by the project manager as a guide to indicate where he should be spending his management time. It is probably the best application of the variability concepts discussed in the previous sections.

SUMMARY

Network planning techniques are proven aids for the project manager. The complete project manager knows that techniques such as PERT are not a panacea for most management problems. The complete project manager uses the technique as a way of structuring thinking, in addition to the normal tasks of planning and control. As a result of such thinking, the complete project manager, in addition to all other team members, is aware of which activities are on the critical path, which activities are on any shadow critical path and which activities have slack. The complete project manager uses this information to classify activities in a triage fashion for levels of management attention. In this way, the complete project manager uses PERT "judiciously."

GUIDE TO FURTHER READING

This chapter has presented the essentials of constructing network diagrams and bar charts as well as reviewing the PERT process. The CPM and other network-based techniques will be covered in Chapter 4. At this point, the reader may wish to examine more detail of both the techniques and their application. The references are thus divided into two parts: part I lists those which discuss network techniques in more detail, and part II lists some reported applications of these techniques.

REFERENCES

Part I—Techniques

Archibald, R. D. and Villoria, R. L. *Network Based Management System (PERT/CPM)*. New York: John Wiley & Sons, 1967.

Battersby, A. *Network Analysis for Planning and Scheduling*. New York: Macmillan and Company, 1967.

Goyol, S. K. "A Note on a Simple CPM Time-Cost Tradeoff Algorithm," *Management Science,* February 1975.

Levin, R. I. and Kirkpatrick, C. A. *Planning and Control with PERT/CPM*. New York: McGraw-Hill, 1966.

Lockeyer, K. G. *An Introduction to Critical Path Analysis*. New York: American Management Association, 1964.

Miller, R. W. *Schedule, Cost and Profit Control with PERT.* New York: McGraw-Hill, 1963.

Moder, J. J. "Network Techniques in Project Management" in *Project Management Handbook* (D. Cleland and W. King, Eds.). New York: Van Nostrand Reinhold, 1983.

Moder, J. J. and Phillips, C. P. *Project Management with PERT and CPM,* New York: Reinhold Publishing Company, 1964.

Wiest, J. D. and Levy, F. K. *A Management Guide to PERT/CPM.* Englewood Cliffs, N.J.: Prentice-Hall, 1977.

Part II—Applications

Antill, J. M. and Woodhead, R. W. *Critical Path Methods in Construction Practice.* New York: Wiley Interscience, 1970.

Boulanger, D. "PERT: A Case Study Application with Analysis," *Advanced Management,* July 1961.

Brennen, J. (Ed.). *Applications of Critical Path Techniques,* London: The English University Press, 1968.

Bruegman, D. C. "Using CPM at a University," *Journal of Systems Management,* January 1973.

Gisser, P. "Taking Chances out of Product Introductions," *Industrial Marketing,* May 1965.

Greenlaw, P. S. "Management Science and Personnel Management," *Personnel Journal,* November 1973.

Hanson, R. S. "Moving the Hospital," *Industrial Engineering,* November 1982.

Jennet, E. "Experience with and Evaluation of Critical Path Methods," *Chemical Engineering,* February 10, 1969.

Odom, R. G. and Blystone, E. A Case Study of CPM in a Manufacturing Situation, *Journal of Industrial Engineering,* November–December 1964.

Schoderbeck, P. P. "A Study of the Applications of PERT," *Journal of Academy Management,* September 1965.

Strenski, J. B. "PERT Charting Public Relations," *Public Relations Journal,* February 1975.

Wahl, R. P., Jr. "PERT Controls Budget Preparation," *Public Management,* February 1964.

Wong, Y. "Critical Path Analysis for New Product Planning," *Journal of Marketing,* October 1964.

4
Additional Project
Planning Techniques

*Beware lest you lose the substance
by grasping at the shadow.*
Aesop's Fables
6th c. B.C.

This chapter reviews additional network-based planning techniques that have been developed either along with, or in addition to, PERT. As the chapter develops, the techniques become increasingly complex and abstract. The reader is cautioned not to look for easy answers to complex problems or to become enamored by the mathematics of these techniques. One should not lose the substance by grasping at the shadow.

The first technique reviewed is the critical path method (CPM), a network-based technique which allows for time and cost trade-offs.

Project resources are considered next, and techniques are reviewed for dealing with the situation in which resources are constrained in some way. The techniques include resource loading diagrams, resource leveling, and resource allocation.

Finally, the Graphical Evaluation and Review Technique (GERT) is reviewed. This network-based technique allows for feedback loops, activity failure, and other contingencies not considered in PERT/CPM.

THE CRITICAL PATH METHOD—CPM

Both PERT and CPM are network-based planning methods. As seen in Chapter 3, PERT is particularly time oriented and seems most

useful when the processes to be used for the project are not well known. Cost is not explicitly considered, although there is always the implicit assumption that time is money. There have been attempts to explicitly consider costs in the PERT process. Such attempts have been labeled PERT/cost technique, and the reader is referred to the article by DeCoster (1964) for details of that technique.

CPM considers cost explicitly but does not include the three time estimates feature of PERT. Thus CPM seems best suited for those projects in which the processes for the activities are fairly well known but the activities have not been done in that sequence before or the project is being done on a new location or with new personnel. New locations and new personnel generally exhibit the weak culture characteristics discussed in Chapter 1.

We begin CPM with the usual network activities of assigning times to activities and then plotting the times and activities as a network. The original times assigned to the activities are considered the "normal" times for those activities. The normal time is the time that each activity would normally take if the activity were staffed and partitioned in the normal way. The normal time is assumed to have a normal cost associated with it.

In addition to the normal time and cost, we also define a crash time and a crash cost. The crash time is considered to be the minimum time in which the activity could be completed. This minimum time is usually accomplished by loading the activity with the maximum amount of assets, such as more men, more machinery, or both. The crash time thus has an associated crash cost, which is usually much higher than the normal cost.

Given the normal time and cost along with the crash time and cost, a figure called the cost slope can now be calculated. The *cost slope* is considered to be the cost per unit of time to reduce the activity duration; it is calculated by dividing the difference between the normal time and the crash time by the difference between the crash cost and the normal cost. For example, if an activity has a normal time of ten weeks and a crash time of eight weeks, then the difference in time is two weeks. One can thus "buy" two weeks on this activity. If the normal cost for this activity is $10,000 and the crash cost is $50,000, then the difference is $40,000. This is how much it will cost to buy the two weeks. The cost slope is thus given as:

$$\text{Cost Slope} = \$40,000/2 = \$20,000$$

This figure is the cost per week of reducing the activity duration. It is assumed that the project manager, or some other decision maker, can buy as many weeks as desired, up to the crash limit, and that the cost for each week will be equal to the cost slope. Thus if the project manager in this example wanted to reduce the activity by one week, that could be done at a cost of $20,000. If it was desired to reduce the activity duration by two weeks, that could be done at a cost of $40,000.

The essence of the critical path method is to examine all options for reducing the total project duration. The method begins by examining the minimum cost options and proceeds through to the maximum cost options. All of the options are then listed in the order of increasing cost of reducing the project duration by one week. The options are then presented to the decision maker. The method does not propose any "best" solution. The method is illustrated in the following section by way of example.

A CPM Example

The first step is to construct a table listing each activity, its predecessor activity, and its associated normal time, crash time, normal cost, crash cost, and cost slope. Such a table for the sample problem in Chapter 3 is given in Table 4-1.

The next step is to construct a network diagram giving the normal times, to find the critical path, and to compute the total cost using the

Table 4-1. Data for CPM Example.

| ACTIVITY | PREDECESSORS | NORMAL | | CRASH | | COST |
		DAYS	$(000)	DAYS	$(000)	SLOPE $(000)
a	—	5	10	3	20	5
b	a	6	15	5	17	2
c	b	10	10	7	13	1
d	b	4	5	3	8	3
e	c	5	20	—	—	—
f	d	9	25	8	26	1
g	e,f	10	15	8	35	10
h	g	5	10	—	—	—
i	g	6	12	4	38	13
j	h,i	5	10	4	50	40

normal costs for all activities. This is called the base case and is shown in Figure 4-1.

The next step is to determine the minimum cost option for reducing the total project duration by one day. Examining Table 4-1, we see that there are two activities that have a cost slope of $1,000, activities c and f. However, activity f is not on the critical path (see Figure 4-1) so investing assets in this activity will only increase costs without decreasing project duration. Thus the decision at this point would be to reduce activity c by one day at a cost of $1,000.

Having made that decision, we must next examine its effect on our network diagram to see if the critical path has changed. This is shown in Figure 4-2. In this case, the reduction of one day in activity c did not affect the location of the critical path. The current revised case is scheduled to be completed in 46 days instead of the original 47 days.

We are now set to return to Table 4-1 in order to look for the next reduction. Again we see that activity c represents the least cost way of reducing total project duration. At this point, we make the decision to reduce activity c by an additional day. The effect of this on the network diagram is shown in Figure 4-3. With this revision, we see that the critical path has changed. There is now a dual critical path proceeding through activities d and f. Dual critical paths appear when there are two critical paths that have the same duration. Now although there is still one day available for activity c, the entire project duration cannot be reduced simply by reducing that activity. This is because the dual critical path must now also be reduced in order to have any effect on the total project duration. We must now consider reducing an activity on each of the critical paths.

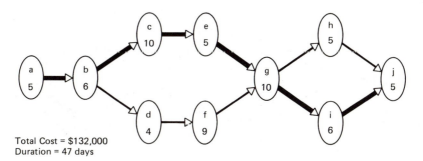

Total Cost = $132,000
Duration = 47 days

Figure 4-1. Base Case for CPM Example.

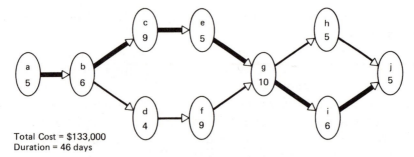

Total Cost = $133,000
Duration = 46 days

Figure 4-2. Revised Case for CPM Example.

Examining Table 4-1, we see that the least cost combination is to reduce activities c and f by one day each for a total cost of $2,000. Searching a bit further, however, we see that an alternative is to reduce activity b by one day for the same price of $2,000. From a mathematical standpoint, it could be said that the project manager would be indifferent about which of the two choices was made. The mathematical result is the same either way. However, from a managerial viewpoint, there may be a strong tendency towards reducing the single activity b rather than the combination of c and f. This could be due to the feeling that all crashing increases the need for management effort. Crashing also seems to increase everyone's level of anxiety and the chances for problems to develop. In addition, it would seem to be advantageous to save time as early in the job as possible. Thus, at this point it would seem best to choose activity b for crashing.

Choosing activity b does not affect the critical path, but it does add $2,000 to the cost. So at this point the project stands at 44 days' dura-

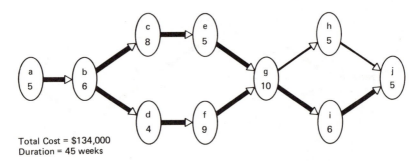

Total Cost = $134,000
Duration = 45 weeks

Figure 4-3. Revised Case for CPM Example.

tion for a cost of $136,000. Since activity b can only be reduced by one day, in order to continue to reduce project duration, the combination of activities c and f must now be used. Doing this does not change the location of the critical path, but it does reduce its length and adds another $2,000 to the total cost. Thus after this decision, the project stands at 43 days' duration for a cost of $138,000.

The CPM method continues to select activities for reduction until the project duration can no longer be reduced. The reader should be able to verify using the data from Table 4-1 that the following activities would be chosen in the order:

a	2 days
g	2 days
i	1 day
j	1 day

After these choices, activities d and i would still have days available, but such reductions would have no effect on the project's duration. The final network diagram is given in Figure 4-4.

Management Review of CPM Results

It should be clear from a management standpoint that Figure 4-4 does not necessarily represent "the answer" to the sample problem but rather "an answer" that is mathematically feasible. The CPM process does not consider whether or not the maximum crash answer is managerially feasible, and many managers agree it is not. As in most cases in life where a dichotomy is presented—here the dichotomy be-

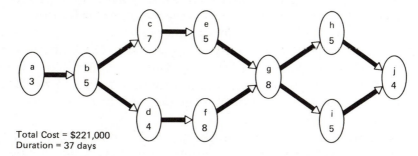

Total Cost = $221,000
Duration = 37 days

Figure 4-4. Final Case for CPM Example.

ing between no crash and maximum crash—the answer probably lies somewhere in between.

The CPM process presents an array of possible answers. Selecting the plan to be implemented requires managerial judgment. Usually, only top management can determine how much a day's reduction in the schedule is worth to the organization. It may be determined that the project absolutely must be done in 43 days. In this case, activity c would be reduced by three days and activities b and f would each be reduced by one day. On the other hand, management may feel that any schedule reduction is only worth $1,000 per day. In this case, only activity c would be reduced by two days. The actual schedule is a judgment call.

The project manager should beware of solutions approaching the maximum crash situation. Indeed the sample project can be completed in 37 days, and top management may set that figure, perhaps in order to "stretch" the project team. However, that solution has everyone moving at full speed and almost any delay would cause problems. Any system can only operate at maximum capacity for a short period of time. After that, systems tend to disintegrate rapidly and no amount of management energy can stop the process. The "full tilt" solution is usually feasible only on paper.

What CPM does do well is to point out rapidly those activities where the schedule can be reduced at minimum cost. Many times, managers are not aware of just how cheaply time can be reduced on a project. Adding more assets to one or two activities can often gain several weeks. Finding the few activities that make a large difference is the most important advantage of using the critical path method.

Davis (1974) indicates that although CPM or other time/cost trade-off procedures are useful for management, they have not been widely implemented in practice. He states that the major reason for this lies in the amount and complexity of input data required for analysis, coupled with the typical uncertainty of these data. The collection of detailed time/cost data for projects consisting of hundreds of activities, for example, is not an easy task. In addition, data are not free, and the cost associated with their collection must be weighed against the potential benefits expected.

If we agree that the real benefit from CPM is in finding those few activities that will cheaply buy us time, then there is an apparent answer to the problem of data costs. The trick is to collect data only for those activities that are critical or are on any shadow critical paths, which is a path with duration close to the calculated critical path. Since these are the activities that determine project duration, it is clear that the few activities we are looking for will be found among these. Other activities may be treated as if they cannot be crashed, or they can be assigned arbitrarily large costs. When this is done, only the first few iterations through the procedure will be valid, but then those are probably the only ones that are really necessary for decision making purposes.

RESOURCE ALLOCATION PROCEDURES

Another criticism typically leveled at network planning procedures is that they are somewhat naive models of most real-life situations in that they focus on time and cost, and do not consider the constraints of resource requirements and availabilities. Often, the resource availability is a more important factor in scheduling an activity than is the time or cost of that activity. With this in mind, we now examine some of the basic procedures that have been developed to deal with the resource allocation problem.

Resource Loading Diagrams

One of the chief tools of resource scheduling is a resource loading diagram. Such a diagram plots the level of a given resource usage over time as the project proceeds. The resources plotted can be money, unskilled manpower, particular skills required, or particular machinery. The diagram is usually derived from the bar chart associated with the project and a knowledge of the skills or other resources needed for each activity. Each diagram pertains to a given resource, so separate diagrams are needed if several resources are being scheduled.

As an example, the sample problem of Chapter 3 is extended below by adding a new activity k with a time of ten days. This activity can be done at any time during the project. The bar chart associated with the extended sample problem is shown in Figure 4–5.

For this problem, the resource we will be concerned with is cash. We assume that there is one person working on each activity and that cash requirements are $100 per person per day. After the activities have been scheduled, the resource loading diagram can be derived by counting the number of activities that are being performed each day and then multiplying by the cash needs figure of $100. A resource

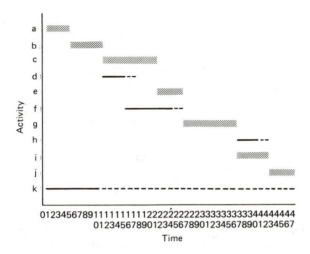

Figure 4-5. Bar Chart for Extended Sample Problem.

loading diagram for the extended sample problem is shown in Figure 4-6. For this example, it is assumed that all activities are scheduled to begin on their early start times.

Most of the simple resource scheduling techniques involve manipulating the noncritical activities on the bar chart in order to change the resource loading schedule in some way. For example, suppose that members of the finance department were to see the charts in Figures 4-5 and 4-6. They would probably ask if the schedule could be changed so that the cash was spent as late as possible. They might argue that this would be good because the organization could earn the maximum amount of interest from its cash balances. Given this constraint, the bar chart and resource loading diagram would be rearranged as shown in Figures 4-7 and 4-8. The changes would be simply to schedule all activities with slack to begin at their late start times.

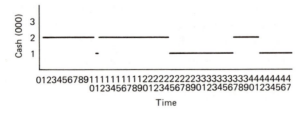

Figure 4-6. Resource Loading Diagram for Figure 4-5.

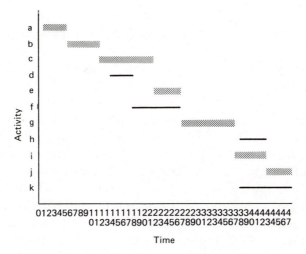

Figure 4-7. Bar Chart for Latest Cash Outlay.

Resource Leveling

In many project scheduling situations, the schedule of resource demands may not be of major concern because ample quantities of the required resources are available. However, it may be that the pattern of resource usage has undesirable features, such as frequent changes in the amount of a particular resource desired. Resource leveling techniques are useful here to provide a means of distributing resource usage over time to minimize the period-by-period variations in the resource of interest.

Resource leveling also involves rescheduling of the activities with slack, but this time with a goal of minimizing the number of jumps in the resource loading chart. Figure 4-8 shows four jumps in resource

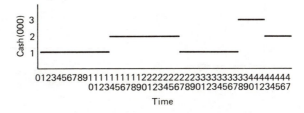

Figure 4-8. Resource Loading Diagram for Figure 4-7.

usage, one of them from $100 to $300 per day. Suppose now that it is desired to have as few jumps as possible, with none of them to the $300 level. This can be accomplished by scheduling activity k to be done at the same time as activity g and by scheduling activity h at its early start time. The resulting charts are shown in Figures 4–9 and 4–10.

A different type of resource leveling problem arises when there is a fixed resource constraint. Suppose for our example that there was a constraint on cash outlays such that the level could not rise above $200 per day. Sometimes the problem can be leveled within that type of constraint, as shown in Figure 4–10. However, such happy results are not always the case. Suppose, for example, that activity k could not begin until activity g was completed. This would be similar to the case given in Figure 4–7. However, the associated resource loading diagram shows that the $200 constraint will be violated. If that constraint cannot be changed, then there is no other option than to lengthen the completion time of the project. The solution with extended time would be for activity i to begin after activity h. Then activity k could be scheduled to be done while h and i were also being completed. This constraint would add five days to the schedule, as shown in Figure 4–11, with resource loading diagram shown in Figure 4–12.

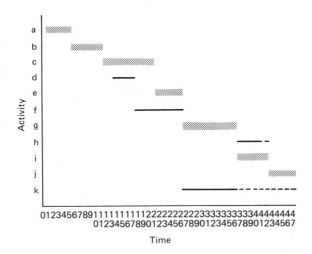

Figure 4-9. Bar Chart for Resource Leveling.

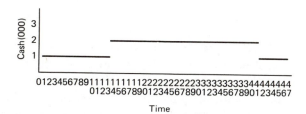

Figure 4-10. Resource Loading Diagram for Figure 4-9.

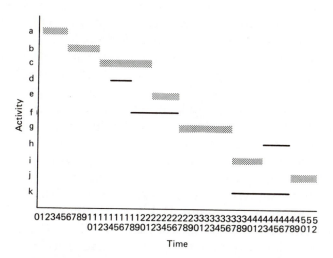

Figure 4-11. Bar Chart for Constrained Cash Problem.

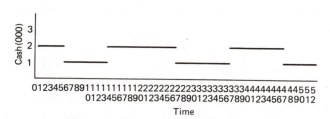

Figure 4-12. Resource Loading Diagram for Figure 4-11.

Scheduling Heuristics

As indicated by these simple examples, constrained resource scheduling is not an exact science. It is often a matter of juggling and switching activities until a resource-feasible solution emerges. For the examples, this could be done by eyesight. For real-life problems, that is not usually possible. As an aid in more complex problems, approximate procedures called heuristics (or rules of thumb) have been developed to help the scheduler examine the myriad of combinations that are possible.

In resource-constrained projects, the basic problem is that two activities need the same resource and there is not enough of that resource to satisfy both. The question then becomes one of determining which activity will be delayed. A heuristic is basically a decision rule that can be used to make the choice. Each decision rule has both positive and negative consequences. For example, the best known rule is probably "first come—first served." This has the positive consequence of treating all activities fairly and being easy to administer. However, it could have the negative consequence of possibly picking a noncritical job over a critical one simply because it asked for the asset first.

As might be suspected, there are different heuristics that work well under different sets of circumstances. Other heuristics that have been studied include: shortest operation first, minimum slack first, minimum operation first, maximum slack first, minimum total work content first, and maximum total work content first. There is a fairly comprehensive and complex body of knowledge which defines the "best" heuristics for a given set of circumstances. The interested reader is referred to articles by Talbot (1982) and by Kurtulus and Davis (1982) for further details.

In reality, most resource-constrained scheduling is done using routines supplied with network technique computer programs. However, the project manager should be aware of which rule is being used to arrive at the resource-constrained schedule. This is handy to know because most resource-constrained *work* may actually be done using some other heuristic, perhaps the "squeaky wheel" rule. Thus the work often does not match the schedule. To understand this problem better, a somewhat humorous account of how production scheduling is really done appears in the end-of-chapter reading (Woolsey, 1982).

Summary of Resource Allocation Procedures

There are several approaches to the resource allocation problem. With ordinary PERT and CPM, no explicit consideration of resources is made. Consideration of resource problems has led to:

Resource Loading Diagrams	For each resource, a total resource requirement profile is calculated by summing, period by period, requirements of that resource for all activities as they occur in an early start (or any other) schedule. No rescheduling is involved.
Resource Leveling Procedures	Using the resource loading diagrams with the early start schedule, one attempts to reduce peak requirements by shifting slack jobs to nonpeak periods. Resource limits are not given. The objective is to smooth resource usage without delaying the project completion.
Resource Allocation Procedures	Here, resource levels are fixed and project completion may be delayed. The fixed resources are allocated to available jobs according to scheduling heuristics that determine which jobs will be postponed when total requirements exceed resources.

PROBABILISTIC NETWORK TECHNIQUES—GERT

One of the criticisms often leveled at PERT/CPM techniques is that they are deterministic. That is, it is predetermined which activities will be done to complete a certain project. It is assumed that all activities on the network chart will be done, sooner or later, and that the completion of all activities marks the end of the project. Duration of an activity is the only area of uncertainty that is considered.

For many types of projects, particularly those in which the processes are not well known, there are many other areas of uncertainty to be considered. For example, an activity in a software development project might be to "test program results." Succeeding activities normally assume that the program results tested well and that the program thus works. However, this is not always the case. The program results may not test at all, and it may not be known if this represents a software error, a hardware error, or a little bit of both. Even worse, it may be that the problem specifications were improperly designated so that the project needs to return to some previous stage of problem specification design.

These contingencies of looping "back to the drawing boards" for redesign or respecification are common in development projects. However, PERT/CPM networks require that all jobs must be successfully completed. No allowance is made for looping back to a previous activity or for outright activity or project failure.

To compensate for these deficiencies, more generalized networking systems have been developed. Probably the best known of these systems is called the Graphical Evaluation and Review Technique (GERT).

These more generalized systems normally use AoA notation and make use of probabilistic nodes or probabilistic events. With deterministic nodes, every node is eventually reached or *released*. This happens when all jobs leading into that node have been completed. Similarly, all activities emanating from a given node may start only after that node has been released, and all of them must eventually be completed.

With probabilistic networks, all nodes are not necessarily reached. Thus all activities are not necessarily completed. Each node allows for probabilistic exits from that node such that only one of several emanating activities will actually be performed. Likewise, certain nodes may be released when one or more, but not necessarily all, of the activities leading into them are completed. Thus this system allows for branching, looping, and for probabilities of activities even occurring.

With GERT, each node is considered to have an input side on the left and an output side on the right. Each side represents certain logical relations with respect to connecting activities. In general, the input side specifies how many incoming activity completions are required for the first release of the node and then for subsequent releases of the node. The existence of the subsequent releases of a node allows for cycles and feedback loops to be represented by a network diagram.

Two types of output sides are used. The different types determine the type of branching that occurs from the node. Deterministic branching is used when all activities will be completed, the same as the normal PERT/CPM diagram. Probabilistic branching is used when one of several emanating activities is to be performed.

Symbols for the input and output sides of the nodes are given as follows [from Pritsker and Sigel (1974)]:

SYMBOL	MEANING
Input	
$\left(\begin{array}{c} m \\ \hline n \end{array}\right.$	The first nodal release will occur when there have been m incident activity completions. Subsequent releases require n completions.
$\left(\begin{array}{c} m \\ A \\ n \end{array}\right\rangle$	The first nodal release requires that m different incident activities be completed. Subsequent releases require n such completions.
$\left(\begin{array}{c} m \\ H \\ n \end{array}\right\rangle$	The first nodal release will occur with m incident activity completions. All other ongoing incident activities will be halted at that point. Subsequent releases require n completions, with the same halting conditions.
$\left(\begin{array}{c} m \\ U \\ \bar{n} \end{array}\right\rangle$	The first nodal release requires m different incident activities to be completed. All other ongoing incident activities will be halted at that point. Subsequent releases require n such completions, with the same halting conditions.
Output	
$\left. j \right)$	Deterministic branching node. Upon release of node j, all jobs emanating from the node will be initiated.
$j \triangleright$	Probabilistic branching node. Upon release of node j, one of the emanating activities will be initiated.

An Example of GERT Networks

The following example of using GERT for multiteam, multiproject research and development planning is taken from an article by Moore and Taylor (1977):*

3.1. *The Prototype Model*

Prior to development of the overall model, a prototype model was developed for a subset of the overall system. This was done to reflect the elements common to all four R & D projects. Each of the four research and development projects was described by five basic stages as follows: (1) problem definition, (2) research activity, (3) solution proposal, (4) prototype development, and (5) solution implementation.

A GERT network for the above-described R & D process is shown as one of the four subsystems in Figure 1, a complete schematic of the multiproject, multiteam system. By observing nodes 10 through 17 in this network, one can identify the five-stage R & D model for one project. While the sequential nature of the five-stage R & D process is left intact, the possibilities of repeating stages as well as two possible outcomes leading to project termination have been shown.

Upon completion of the initial stage, problem definition, stage 2—research activity—is normally initiated. However, for the firm in question, experience has shown that the problem is frequently insufficiently defined to proceed further. The network reflects this feature of the process by looping back to node 11, according to a predefined probability. (Probabilities are assigned to each of the branching alternatives from node 12, with sum 1.0.)

The next major decision point in the prototype model for a single R & D project is at node 14, completion of a solution proposal. There is no loop prior to this (at node 13) since the firm does not evaluate the research activity until the research team has completed its analysis of the research findings and developed a proposal. Four alternatives were identified as possible outcomes to the research and proposal activities. First, although the problem definition was accepted (at node 12), it is concluded at this point that the problem was incorrectly defined, and the network loops back to node 11 for redefinition of the problem. Second, the research results are inconclusive and the network loops back to node 12 for additional research activity (this was, in fact, one of the most frequent causes for extending the time required for the overall R & D project). Third, all research leads to the conclusion that all solutions are infeasible, which results in a "washout" and project termination (network node 17). In terms of prior probability assessment, this

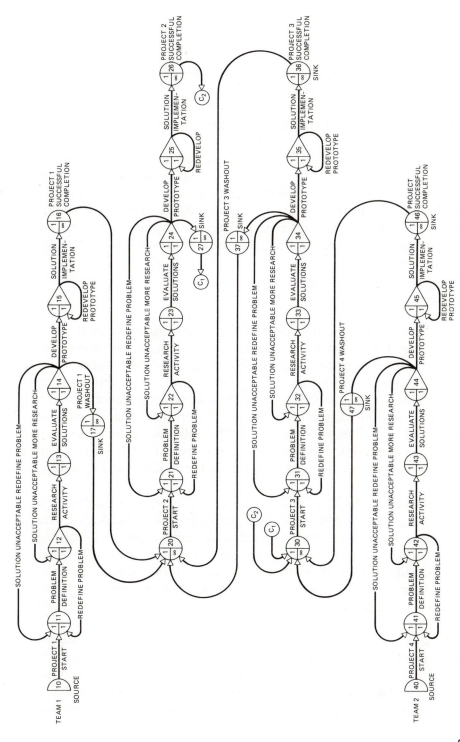

Figure 1. GERT Network of Multiteam, Multiproject Team R & D Process.

81

was the most difficult to estimate. Finally, given that the solution proposal was acceptable, stage 4 would be initiated.

On completion of stage 4—prototype development—the prototype is either redeveloped (self-loop around node 15) or implementation is started. Node 16 denotes successful completion of the R & D project.

By means of simulation, this model was used to generate approximate statistics for the probability of successful completion or washout for each project. Approximate statistics were also generated for the expected project duration and the variance of these durations. The minimum times and maximum times are also noted. Given cost data, the associated cost statistics can also be generated.

MANAGEMENT REVIEW OF ADDITIONAL NETWORK TECHNIQUES

This chapter has reviewed some of the extensions of network techniques that have been developed to solve particular problems. The chapter was not intended to make the manager an expert in these techniques but rather to give an appreciation of what the techniques can and cannot do. At the beginning of the chapter, the reader was cautioned against grasping at the shadows of a problem in an attempt to find simple solutions to complex problems. To successfully use project network models, managers must recognize their strengths and limitations, and not be overly reliant on the models for managerial purposes.

It should be easily recognized that by their very nature, the computer programs written to support the techniques described in this chapter are capable of producing reams of output reports. Because of the existence of such reports, there may be a temptation to overuse this capability and to overstructure the project information and control system. The manager is thus cautioned not to let the contents of the computer-generated form determine what is important for project success.

As an example, the study by Baker et al. (1983) concerning the determinants of project success, noted with concern an increasing emphasis within some corporations on the creation of ". . . elaborate and detailed reporting and control systems [which lead to] excessive delays, red tape, superficial reports, and inadequate information flows." Such overuse tends to detract from project effectiveness. The report becomes more important than project progress. This is the ultimate in grasping at shadows.

On the other side of the coin, CPM has been demonstrated as an effective planning tool if used "judiciously." Resource loading and leveling schemes are also useful for allocation decisions. The complete project manager would consider using both of these tools for project planning.

REFERENCES

Baker, B. N., Murphy, P. C., and Fisher, D. "Factors Affecting Project Success" in *Project Management Handbook,* D. Cleland and W. King (eds.). New York: Van Nostrand Reinhold, 1983.

DeCoster, D. T. "PERT/COST: The Challenge," *Management Services,* May–June, 1964.

Davis, E. W. "Networks: Resource Allocation," *Industrial Engineering,* April 1974.

Kurtulus, I. and Davis, E. W. "Multi-Project Scheduling: Categorization of Heuristic Rules Performance," *Management Science,* February 1982.

Moore, L. J. and Taylor, B. W. III. "Multiteam, Multiproject Research and Development Planning with GERT," *Management Science,* December 1977.

Pritsker, A. A. B. and Sigel, C. E. *The GERT III Z User's Manual.* West Lafayette, Ind.: Pritsker & Associates, 1974.

Talbot, F. B. "Resource-Constrained Project Scheduling with Time-Resource Trade-offs: The Nonpreemptive Case," *Management Science,* October 1982.

Woolsey, G. "The Fifth Column: Production Scheduling as It Really Is," *Interfaces,* **12,** 115–118, December 1982.

THE FIFTH COLUMN:
PRODUCTION SCHEDULING AS IT REALLY IS*

Gene Woolsey

Mineral Economics Department
Colorado School of Mines
Golden, Colorado

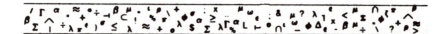

The Push-Down, Pop-Up Principle

One of the basic ideas in all of production scheduling is that of the push-down, pop-up principle. Simply stated this means that if you optimize, say, a job or flow shop according to some particular criterion, you may get what you want and also what you didn't expect.

Another way of stating it is to say that if you push something down, something else will just naturally pop up and bite you on some vulnerable spot. Let us now consider some of the standard methods for scheduling a batch of jobs on one process in light of the principle stated above. We shall assume that all of the jobs have different due dates (in days from now) and different processing times.

SPT, or Shortest Processing Time Rule

This method simply puts the jobs in increasing order of processing time. Technically it does two rather neat things as follows:

—It minimizes the sum of completion times.
—It minimizes the sum of waiting times.

Of course, these things are only possible if we ignore such trivia as promise dates and priorities. Also, I must confess that in my time on mill and shop floors I have yet to have some foreman come up and request that I schedule the machine to do either. The time has come to tell the truth. The above scheduling method is usually known on the factory floor as the "before the auditors come" method.

Say that we are having a typically hellish day out on the floor of the steel service center. The salesmen have told the customary lies about promise dates and we are up to our backsides in the proverbial alligators. In-process inventory is piled up all over the floor, and naturally it is STAINLESS (=

Big Buck$). At this point the floor super gets a phone call from his cousin at corporate HQ telling him that the auditors are coming for a surprise visit and that the in-process had better be acceptably minimal.

Now the production manager is nobody's fool. Any idiot can see that if you schedule the jobs in SPT order you will clear out a lot of short jobs. On this basis your productivity (measured in number of jobs shoved out the door per unit time) will look absolutely super. By the time the ferrets from auditing show up, the floor is clean and new records are being set in jobs out the door per day. Clearly, this is the good news. It does not take long for the push-down, pop-up principle to work, however, as we shall see. What has happened is that our manager has shoved every short, high-value job he has out the door. The bad news is that he now faces the jobs that are left, that is, the long, low-value jobs. In short, he may have set a production record yesterday, but the next few days are really going to be bad news on a due date or priority basis.

DDR, or the Due Date Rule

Any decent textbook on scheduling, such as Conway, Maxwell, and Miller [1967], will tell you that if you schedule a batch of jobs in increasing order of due dates you will minimize the maximum tardiness that can occur. This rule has considerable intuitive appeal as you simply schedule the job next that is due next. Let us, however, consider a case seething with reality. Say that you are the prime supplier of Acapulco Gold to the Detroit Mafia. The Capo de Tutti Capi has politely informed you that the lateness of delivery to any of his boys will be proportional to the size of the goon sent to work you over. A moment's reflection tells you that you wish to minimize the maximum goon that can appear. If you schedule the jobs according to the due date rule, the good news is clearly that nothing will be VERY late. Unfortunately the very bad news is that you have insured a high probability that EVERYTHING is late. In terms of our story, it is cheerfully admitted that all of the goons are midgets but if they ALL hit you in the knee, you still are in a world of hurt.

Minimizing the Number of Late Jobs: Moore's Rule

This method, at first blush, sounds like the answer to a scheduler's prayer. Who wouldn't want to minimize the number of late jobs. It just sounds too good to be true, or useful, in reality (and it IS). Let's consider the example below taken from an earlier effort of mine [Woolsey and Swanson 1975]. We have six jobs with due dates and processing times as shown:

Job Number	1	2	3	4	5	6
Due Date	9	13	16	22	35	40
Production Time	6	8	4	7	21	11

We note that Moore's Method states that first we must put the jobs in due date order. Recall that this says nothing will be very late but everything CAN be late. We then start doing the jobs until we create a late job. When one is found, we look at all the jobs up to and including the late one, pick off the job with the biggest processing time and put it dead last. If we apply this rule to the above set of jobs we come to the sequence below:

Job Number	1	3	4	6	2	5
Due Date	9	16	22	40	13	35
Production Time	6	4	7	11	8	21
Total Time	6	10	17	28	36	57

It doesn't take a genius to see that the good news is certainly that you have maximized on time performance. You also don't have to be too smart to see that you have, for sure, lost two customers forever. Clearly this is a method to use only if your spouse is gainfully employed and makes more than you do.

SLACK: The Slack Rule

The slack rule is a real weirdo among scheduling rules. It assures you that it will maximize the minimum tardiness that can occur for a batch of jobs. Your first reaction should be: "Why in the devil would anyone be crazy enough to do that?" This reaction is caused by your perception of the statement above. If I tell you that I am going to "maximize the minimum tardiness," What you *hear* me say looks like this:

"MAXIMIZE the minimum tardiness."

And that sounds bad.

Recall that when I told you that the due date rule would "minimize the maximum tardiness." What you *heard* then looked like this:

"MINIMIZE the maximum tardiness."

And that sounded good.

Another simple way to state this is: This method will find the sequence of jobs that makes the least tardy job as late as possible. Now, stated like that it seems even worse. This is clearly an example of a scheduling method where the pop-up seems to be more evident than the push-down. Let us now seek out the good news for this method. Consider the two jobs below in the sequences as shown:

Job Number	1	2	2	1
Due Date	10	30	30	10
Production Time	5	5	5	5
Total Time	5	10	5	10

A quick look reveals that both sequences will result in all jobs being on time, *if nothing goes wrong*. As I have said before, this is like saying that the cannon ball will fall right *there* (neglecting air resistance). It is not hard to see which sequence of the two any experienced floor supervisor would choose. He would certainly choose the one that would minimize the chance of any job being late, thus the first sequence. In short, it is a natural human tendency to cover one's behind on any and all occasions. The fact that this method, consistently used, means that, on the average, the least late job is jolly late is a political matter and will not be further discussed here.

Remembrance of Things Past

As Proust [1928] tells us, there are the ways of Swann and the ways of Guermantes, the plain and the aristocratic. A good rule to remember is if you find one of the above methods that fits the apparent problem perfectly, you obviously don't know the political situation. Every one of the methods discussed above works well when sufficient consideration is given to the politics in which the case in question is imbedded. As I never cease telling my students, if you do not learn to deal with the political situation in which the technical problem is imbedded, be assured that *it will deal with you.*

References

Conway, R. W., Maxwell, W. L., and Miller, L. W. 1967, *Theory of Scheduling,* Addison-Wesley Publishing Company, Don Mills, Ontario.

Proust, Marcel 1928, *Swann's Way,* Random House Publishing Company, New York.

Woolsey, R. E. D., and Swanson, H. S. 1975, *Operations Research for Immediate Application—A Quick and Dirty Manual,* Harper & Row Publishing Company, New York.

5
Planning—People Interaction:
Network Techniques and Team Building*

*The girl who can't dance
says the band can't play.*
Yiddish Proverb

Project managers often complain that the reason they cannot achieve the project goal is that they do not have the right people. The argument of this chapter is that good people can be developed, through proper management, as part of a project team. Project managers would benefit by considering project network development as part of a team building process.

Thus, this chapter examines the broader implications of using network techniques as an integral part of the total process of team building and functioning in project management. To do this, a process is outlined which involves team members participating in the network design by first creating the ideal network chart and then negotiating to find a feasible solution that becomes the initial project plan. It is argued that through such a process, people from divergent fields can begin to develop the routine necessary for a smoothly functioning team. In addition, the iterative negotiation process also helps to establish behavioral norms and levels of trust that are needed for effective groups. Finally, building an ideal network and then reviewing the feasible network are shown to be aids in increasing creativity in project design as well as commitment to implement the initial project plan.

---

*An earlier version of this chapter appeared in *Project Management Methods & Studies,* B. V. Dean (ed.), Elsevier Science Publishers B. V. (North Holland), 1985.

INTRODUCTION

In discussing network techniques, many practicing managers state that the most useful result of a network technique is not in the execution of the project but rather in the development of the initial project plan (Brooks, 1975, p. 156). At first glance, this may seem somewhat paradoxical as it is well known that projects rarely proceed according to the initial plan. However, such statements may not be as strange as they initially seem if one views the proper management of the network building process as a technique for team building and development. Typically, project managers spend most of their concern on the details of the actual network technique, with little concern for the group processes that are taking place as people work with the technique. In this chapter, we shall concentrate on just such groups processes and indicate how the project manager can use these processes for maximum benefit.

The emphasis in this chapter will thus be to explore the role of a network building process in project team development. That is, the emphasis will be on the process followed to build the network and on the part the process plays in the development of behavioral patterns and expectations that help to develop a well-functioning team.

A PROJECT MANAGEMENT PROCESS

Complex projects require complex teams where people must continually interact for a long period of time. Most of the early examples of project management came from the construction industry, where the activities were fairly autonomous and could be carried out relatively independently. For more complex projects such as the development of new expertise or new products, there is a great deal of learning involved in each step of the project and the performance of any given current activity often becomes dependent on what was learned during the completion of the last activity. Such a high degree of interdependency requires a very well-functioning and cohesive team.

Complex projects also require a variety of people with a wide range of skills from throughout the organization. These people will normally not be accustomed to working with each other. They have become accustomed to working according to the norms for behavior used in their home departments. A mixed collection of such behavioral patterns and expectations could be counterproductive. For example, members of a production department may have developed norms of behavior that value strict adherence to schedules. Members of a marketing department may favor looser adherence in order to enhance the possibilities for creativity. When members of these two departments are put on the same project team, each may feel that the other's behavior is counterproductive.

Thus, developing a cohesive team requires developing a set of norms for behavior that might be different from the norms the team members are accustomed to using. It is felt that developing behavioral patterns and expectations should be attended to before the project work commences, and that this development can be enhanced by having all the members of the project team work together to build the initial project plan.

A process which many project managers have used instinctively, and which agrees with many management principles (as discussed later), is given as follows:

1. *Initiation.* Once the end of the project has been specified, an initial project team should be assembled, have the goal explained to them, be given a "rough" network diagram as drawn by the project manager, and asked:
   a. Who else should be on the team?
   b. Without concern of budget restrictions, what would each member contribute to the project if he could do whatever he wanted?
2. *Idealization.* From the answers to these questions, the team and the project manager then construct an idealized network—the project network that they would implement if there were no restrictions.
3. *Iteration.* If the idealized network is within budget and satisfies any other resource constraints, then the idealized network becomes the initial project plan and implementation can begin. If the idealized network does not satisfy resource constraints and these constraints cannot be increased, then the team members must develop ways to negotiate with one another, along with the

project manager, to take aspects away from the idealized network. Each aspect taken away becomes another iteration towards a realistic plan.

4. *Implementation*. The process of negotiation continues to iterate until a feasible solution is found. A feasible solution is a network that is operationally viable and satisfies resource constraints. This network becomes the *initial project plan*. When this plan is realized, each member of the team should reiterate his part in the plan. The initial project plan is the plan with which the project execution begins.

SOME ASPECTS OF TEAM DEVELOPMENT

The process just described is itself an idealization and need not, and perhaps cannot, be followed exactly. However, a number of successful projects have used this method by default. This is due to the fact that at the beginning of the project, either the budget was not known or the means for achieving the end result were not clearly specified, or both. Without these guidelines, it is required that the project team first idealize what they would do and then iterate towards a more feasible solution. These are two important aspects of the process, and the reasons for their importance will be discussed in subsequent sections.

Project managers often say that they could accomplish any task if only they had the "right" people. One common characteristic of these "right" people is that they can operate with a minimum of instruction and supervision. They seem to know what to do without being told. The ability to operate in this manner is often the result of an individual's enculturation to a clear set of goals and norms for behavior. In a stable situation such as a standing department, the norms are taught through a system of customs which have been developed over many years in the presence of the stable situation. It seems that different functions and departments develop significantly different cultures, even within the same organization. The result is that the corporate culture does not necessarily rule to the extent that one can expect harmony between people from different sections.

When people from different departments are assembled for a project, they form a temporary social system. Because the team is new, there is often no system of customs to indicate proper behavior while working on that project. Each person brings his own set of customs, beliefs, and perceptions to the project, and this may not lead to a coherent team culture. Without such a culture, people will behave as if they were "back home" and such behavior could be in conflict with the smooth operation of the project. It is important that the project manager address the problem of "back home" behavior before the project begins. For example, one of the main functions of military indoctrination programs is to eliminate "back home" behavior while the person is acting in a military capacity. This is because "back home" behavior is not appropriate in many military functions. The same may be true for proper project functioning. Thus, the development of a team culture to be used while people are working on a project becomes a prime management consideration during the project planning stage.

To clarify the idea of developing a group culture, consider some of the concepts of culture as developed in the field of anthropology. Many older theories of culture (Durkheim, 1938; Radcliffe-Brown, 1952) assumed the concept of the "group mind," a common set of objectives and motives shared by a group of people, which fostered the cohesiveness and solidarity of that group. It was assumed that most behavior was done for the good of the whole and that this was so because of commonality of motives shared by the members of the society. On a project team, there may be one shared motive—finishing the project. However, this may be the only motive held in common. The project manager cannot rely on commonality of motives for the development of a team culture.

For most recurring purposes, people develop standards for behavior which then become routine within that group. Goodenough (1971, p. 22) defines the operating culture of a group as the set of standards attributed to a group which the individual uses when he is operating with or within that group. This definition would indicate that the project manager should concentrate on standards of behavior, rather than on motives, in order to develop the group operating culture.

In a formal organization, the most important operating culture for an individual comes from the group with which the person has the most contact, generally the department of which the individual is a member. Organizational departments normally have a fairly stable social structure and execute a somewhat repetitive set of tasks. These conditions foster the development of departmental operating cultures. However, when people from different departments are assembled into a special project team, there is no operating culture for the project team, and people will rely on the routines of their respective departmental cultures. In some cases, these standards may be sufficient for executing the task of the project team. In many cases, however, this seems to lead to a patchwork of differing and even contradictory sets of beliefs and subsequent behaviors. It thus seems important for a project manager to develop an operating culture for the project team.

Yet how is this to be done in a heterogeneous group where one cannot assume a commonality of motives? Wallace (1970) concludes that it is not necessary for all members of a group to have the same set of beliefs and motives in order to select the correct behavior under various circumstances. All they need to do is to be able to predict the others' behavior. Wallace sees the unifying mechanism as the perception of equivalent mutual expectancies. These expectancies involve the recognition that the behavior of other people is predictable under various circumstances, regardless of knowledge of their motivation. This predictable behavior is thus capable of being predictably related to one's own actions. Such a system of equivalent mutual expectancies is termed an implicit contract. As an example of the implicit contract, Wallace (1970, p. 34) points out that

The relationship between the driver of a bus and the riders is a contractual one, involving specific and detailed mutual expectancies. The motives of drivers and riders may be as diverse as one wishes; the contract establishes the system.

Wallace goes further by stating that many human endeavors often require nonsharing of certain motivations and ideas among participants in a variety of institutional arrangements. This nonsharing serves two important functions. First, it permits a more complex system to arise than most, or any, of its participants can comprehend. Second, it relieves the participants in a system of the heavy burden of learning and knowing each other's motivations.

With this in mind, the stance taken here is that the participatory process of developing a project network is an important step in creating a project culture. The initial project plan is the explicit contract for the team. Working towards building that network helps to develop the implicit contracts which are necessary for a smoothly working team; that is, it helps to set up the routines and mutual expectancies. Since most projects are quite complex, some nonsharing of procedures will be necessary. That is, it is not necessary for participants to explain exactly how each activity will be completed; it is only necessary that they negotiate for the definition of the end product of each activity along with the assets and time that will be allotted to each activity.

During the process of negotiation, people's assumptions and propositions concerning various aspects of the project will be tested. Some of these will be assumed to be true. This will give rise to a set of beliefs concerning the goal of the project and the goals of the other people who will be working on the project team. These beliefs will in turn give rise to a system of customs that will be used to indicate proper behavior while working on the project. That is, the interaction of members of the project team will become routine. This is the way that the project culture can be created.

The project manager should insure that the culture created fosters the development of an effective group. We thus turn to an examination of the attributes to be fostered in order to increase effectiveness.

ATTRIBUTES OF EFFECTIVE GROUPS

There have been many attributes of groups defined in the literature. Three attributes, however, seem to be common to all definitions:

1. Members perceive themselves as a group, and they know who is in the group and who is not in the group.
2. There is at least one objective upon which all members agree, although each individual member may have a multitude of other objectives.
3. There is a need for interaction because of the interdependencies of the people in the group as they work towards the agreed-upon objective.

Perception of Team Membership

A project team working collaboratively on a network plan should certainly fit the definition of a group. It is assumed here that there is initially some idea of the activities that need to be completed during the project and that the people who are going to manage these activities are brought together for an initial meeting of the project team. In this way, it is revealed who is on the team and who is not on the team. As the planning continues, some people may be added or deleted, but this should be done with the full knowledge of all members of the team. It is rare that any complex project finishes with the same team members with which it began. In order to keep true to the concept that the members perceive themselves as a group, it is important that all members be aware of any changes in group membership as the project planning proceeds.

Group Size and Definition.   A comment should be made here concerning group size. It has been suggested that the first stage of the participation process should include idealized design, where team members consider the project plan without regard to constraints on assets. This could lead to an initial project team that is quite large in size. Lewenstein (1971) notes that the larger the group, the greater is the diversity of talent, skills, and knowledge, and the riskier are the decisions the group is willing to make. Larger groups tend to be more heterogeneous, and studies indicate that heterogeneous groups tend to be more productive than homogeneous groups (Schutz, 1958). The trade-off for the benefits of larger groups is that in larger groups there is less chance of individual participation. "The 'neglected resource' is a common feature of groups, the retiring expert whose views are never heard or never noticed because his participation level is so low" (Handy, 1982, p. 152).

However, using the network diagram as the focal point of the group's activities may help alleviate the nonparticipation problem and thus obviate the problem of size while accruing the benefits. At the initial meeting of the team, each person should discuss how he could help the team towards its objectives. As the network begins to take shape, each person begins to negotiate for activities and assets. When the network is complete, each person should review and explain to the others what he has contributed to the project. In this way, participation becomes one of the behavioral expectations of the group and pressure will be brought to bear on the "retiring expert" to contribute as much as possible.

Common Objective

The second attribute of the effective group is the common objective. As the members of the group start to perceive themselves as a group, there needs to be some agreement on the common objective. The completed project that defines the end of the network should be the stated common objective of all members of the team. If all team members have a very clear understanding of the final result and agree that this is an objective to be reached, the group will tend to be more effective.

It is well known, however, that most people also bring hidden agendas to groups. Hidden agendas are sets of personal objectives which often have nothing to do with the declared objectives of the group. In most project situations, it is not possible to satisfy all of the individual and group objectives simultaneously. To reach the best combined result, each individual on the team, including the project manager, has to be willing to trade off one objective to reach another. Each individual must be willing to take a risk and be ready to accept a less than optimum outcome for himself. Handy (1982, p. 158) states that this will occur only if the participants can agree on a common objective and if they trust each other. He further states that these conditions will normally only happen if the individuals are given a chance to communicate about objectives and are then allowed to prove that such trust is justified by putting it to the test in some other instance. An exception noted is when there are clear group norms or rules. However, since one of the features of a project team is the initial lack of such norms, the exception does not apply in this case. Thus there is a need to build trust.

Building Trust. The trust needed during project execution can be formed during the negotiation for assets. The negotiation phase is seen as the "other instance" in which people can put each other to the test. By proposing a contribution to a project without consideration of constraints, people may inadvertently reveal their objectives and hidden agendas. When the constraints are applied, then all team members will have to make some trade-offs. The ability to make the trade-offs, and to stay true to them, will influence the level of trust that each person has in the others during the execution of the project. If this process is well managed, and if the project manager insures that all trade-offs are strictly adhered to, the level of trust can be quite high.

The negotiation process is also important for establishing the implicit contracts that are a central part of the project culture. It is during negotiation for assets that each person finds out what makes the others tick, and this sets up behavioral patterns that will last for the duration of the project.

Interdependencies

The third attribute listed for effective groups is the recognition of the interdependencies of people for the completion of both the individual activities and the project as a whole. The vivid, graphic display of interdependencies has long been known as one of the main advantages of using network techniques. When an activity is placed in a network, it becomes immediately clear exactly who is dependent on whom in order to begin each activity. In addition, network techniques identify critical activities which are, in essence, those activities that everyone is dependent upon. Thus, focusing on the network is certainly an aid for this aspect of an effective group.

GROUP MATURATION PROCESS

The collaborative procedure of iterating towards an initial project network is supported by Tuckman's (1965) review of group process studies in which group maturity is categorized as having the following four successive stages.

Forming

In the first stage, the group is not yet a group but a set of individuals. This stage is characterized by talk about the purpose of the group, the definition and title of the group, its composition, leadership pattern, and life span. In the case of project management, this stage should be completed by the first or second meeting of the project team in which the objective and participants of the team are introduced and discussed.

Storming

Storming is the conflict stage where the preliminary consensus on purposes, leadership and other roles, norms of work, and behavior is challenged and reestablished. At this stage, a lot of personal agendas are revealed and a certain amount of interpersonal hostility is generated. This stage is particularly important for testing the norms of the group. In the case of project management, this stage is analogous to the stage where team members negotiate for assets and iterate towards the initial project plan.

Norming

In the third stage, the group establishes norms and practices. Norms of functioning of the group are determined, such as when and how it should work, how it should take decisions, and what type of behavior, what level of work, and what degree of openness, trust, and confidence are appropriate. Group members will also determine their level of commitment. In the case of project management, this stage occurs when the initial project plan is completed and each person reviews his part in the plan and commits to the completion of his activities at the level of assets negotiated.

Performing

Performing is the stage in which the plan is executed. Only when the three previous stages have been successfully completed will the group have attained maturity and have the ability to be fully and sensibly productive. It is assumed that there will be changes of the initial project plan during this phase. However, because of level of trust and the implicit contracts built up during the iteration towards the initial project plan, changes should be implemented much more smoothly than if the group were just handed the network chart and told to get to work.

ADDITIONAL BENEFITS OF PARTICIPATORY DESIGN

Two other concepts seem to indicate the benefits of participatory iteration. The first is the interactive planning paradigm given by Ackoff (1974). This paradigm is based on the belief that the principal benefit of planning comes from engaging in it. With this principle, participating in the process is the most important product in planning. A major consequence of participation is seen as a reduction of problems associated with implementing plans. This is based on the feeling that most people would rather be asked than told.

The key to interactive planning is the way that ends and means are selected in it (Ackoff, 1979). This selection is based on the preparation of an idealized design. An idealized network chart consists of what the team members would contribute to a project without regard to budget or other resource constraints. An idealized design is subject to only two constraints. First, it should be technologically feasible, otherwise it could turn out to be science fiction. Secondly, the entire network should be operationally viable, that is, capable of survival if brought into existence.

The remainder of the planning process is directed at approximating this ideal as closely as possible, given the resource constraints and the combination of objectives of people on the project team. The advantages of basing the planning process on such a design have been listed by Ackoff (1979):

1. Team members' thinking expands when they are free from considering financial constraints.
2. Nonconstrained thinking helps people to better realize their own purposes.
3. Expanded thinking helps to ensure that all relevant parties to the project will be included in the project planning.

Another benefit of having team members participate in the network design results from the difference in thought processes between the left and right hemispheres of the human brain. Recent brain research (Bogden, 1969; Carrington, 1978; Ornstein, 1972) has concluded that the left side of the brain is most adept at language, mathematics, and the general analytic and logical type of thinking used in constructing the elements of a network diagram. To complement this, the right side of the brain is more synthetically perceptual, realizing the whole, being able to process many different inputs at once, and recognizing relations and simultaneous dependencies. By concentrating on the details of constructing a network and then standing back to study the entire network, team members exercise both sides of their brain and construct a more complete image of the entire project.

The use of network diagrams seems unique among planning techniques for stimulating this type of whole brain synthesis and subsequent creativity. The network diagram with its indicators of interdependencies shows the entire picture, the gestalt of the situation, in a way that the output of other techniques cannot begin to match. However, in order to get the full benefit, it seems important that team members take the time to look at the network as a whole. It is thus reemphasized that once the initial project plan is constructed, each member of the team should reiterate his part in the plan in the presence of all other team members. In this way, each person can realize how every other activity relates to his own, which is a left brain process, while simultaneously realizing how each activity relates to the whole, thus completing the right brain synthesis.

PROJECT MANAGEMENT AND LEADERSHIP STYLE

Up to this point, we have been concentrating on the behavior of the individual team members. However, a change in team members' behavior necessitates a change in the project manager's leadership style. The examination of leadership style is motivated by a comment by Pearson and Davies (1981) concerning the value of network techniques. They claim,

> It can be argued that some of these techniques are very valuable aids to project managers and to individual team members if seen as components of leadership style.

The basic assumption in dealing with leadership style is that project management is more the management of the team than the management of the tasks. It has been argued that the team goes through various stages in its development and maturity. Pearson and Davies argue that there is a different leadership style appropriate for these different levels of group development. That is, if a project manager finds a group with a given level of maturity, then he should exhibit a particular management style. The results of their study can also be used in a process context: that is, as the group matures, the project manager should shift styles from one level to the next. It will be argued that this process framework indicates that a different management style may be appropriate for the four different steps of the team development process.

The Pearson and Davies' (1981) studies draw heavily on the framework of leadership styles developed by Hershey and Blanchard (1977). This framework posits four levels of task-relevant maturity of any group, going from level M1, the lowest level of task-relevant maturity, to M4, the highest. At level M1, the group cannot accomplish the task without direct supervision. At level M4, the group has matured to accomplish the task with a minimum of supervision.

Four corresponding leadership styles have been outlined by Pearson and Davies' (1981):

S-1—*Structuring.* Organize and direct the work of others, make each person accountable for specific activities, and motivate by demonstrating what needs to be done. With this leadership style, the network chart is "handed down" to the team.

S-2—*Coaching.* Set high but realistic standards of performance, explain what needs to be done, and motivate by giving feedback and being personally involved. With this leadership style, the network is "jointly drawn" by the team and the manager.

S-3—*Encouraging.* Recognize and praise good work, be open and supportive, and motivate by letting others structure work. With this leadership style, the network is "follower drawn" by the team itself.

S-4—*Delegating.* Assign task responsibilities, and let others carry them out. Motivate by giving control and showing respect. This leadership style is most appropriate for the execution of the project where emphasis is on meeting scheduled milestones.

These four categories of leadership style can be seen to correspond with the four steps of the project management process previously developed. The first step suggests that the project manager provide a

Table 5–1. Process, Team Development, and Leadership Behavior Summary.

PROJECT MANAGEMENT PROCESS	TEAM DEVELOPMENT STAGES	LEADERSHIP BEHAVIOR
1. *Initiation:* decide who is on team. What is contribution of each member? Rough outline given by project manager.	*Forming:* group decides purpose, composition, leadership patterns, and life span.	*Structuring:* organize and direct work of others. Produce rough outline of project.
2. *Idealization:* team constructs ideal network diagram.	*Storming:* initial conflict stage. People reveal hidden agendas.	*Coaching:* set high standards. Network jointly drawn.
3. *Iteration:* negotiate for assets to move to initial project plan.	*Norming:* the group establishes degrees of openness, trust, and confidence.	*Encouraging:* let others structure work. Network is follower drawn.
4. *Implementation:* feasible solution found. Execution of project plan begins.	*Performing:* the group is now mature. Project execution begins.	*Delegating:* assign task responsibilities; let others carry them out.

"rough" network diagram in order to introduce the task to the team members. At this point, the team will have very low task maturity so the network is essentially "handed down." The next step suggests that the team and the project manager construct an idealized design, which allows the group to mature by working on a network that is jointly drawn. In step three, the responsibility shifts more to the team members as they negotiate for assets. At the end, they all review—with the project manager and with each other—their parts in the project. With such agreement, the initial project network has been essentially drawn up by the team. With step four, the project commences with a high degree of task maturity in the group. The project can now proceed with a minimum of direct supervision by the project manager. A comparison of the project management process, the stages of group development, and the styles of leadership is given in Table 5–1.

CONCLUSION

Throughout this chapter it has been argued that the process used for designing a project network may often be more important than the network itself. A process was presented in which all project team members work together to build the initial project plan. This is devised by first building the ideal plan, without regard to budget or other resource constraints, and then having team members negotiate towards a feasible project plan. It was argued that such a scheme will (1) help to build a project culture while team members become accustomed to working together, (2) help to build a more effective team as members begin to trust one another, and (3) help to release large amounts of creativity as team members idealize and use both left and right brain activities. With these arguments, it seems important that in the future, the complete project manager will pay more attention to the team building aspects of network planning techniques.

REFERENCES

Ackoff, R. L. *Redesigning the Future.* New York: John Wiley & Sons, 1974.

Ackoff, R. L. "Resurrecting the Future of Operational Research," *J. Op. Res. Soc.,* **30,** 189–199, 1979.

Bogden, J. E., "The Other Side of the Brain: An Appositional Mind," *Bulletin of the Los Angeles Neurological Societies,* **34:** 135–162, July 1969.

Brooks, F. P., Jr. The Mythical Man-Month: Essays on Software Engineering. Reading, Mass.: Addison Wesley, 1975.

Carrington, P. *Freedom in Meditation.* New York: Doubleday, 1978.

Durkheim, E. *The Rules of Sociological Method* (orig. 1895). New York: Free Press, 1938.

Foster, G. M. *Traditional Cultures and the Impact of Technological Change.* New York: Harper, 1962.

Goodenough, W. H. *Culture, Language and Society.* Reading, Mass.: Addison Wesley Modular Publications, No. 7, 1971.

Handy, C. B. *Understanding Organizations.* Harmondsworth, England: Penguin Books, Ltd., 1982.

Harrison, R. How to Describe Your Organization," *Harvard Business Review,* September–October 1972.

Hershey, P. and Blanchard, K. *Management of Organizational Behavior* (3rd ed.). Englewood Cliffs, N.J.: Prentice Hall, 1977.

Lewenstein, E. R. "Group Size and Decision Making Committees," *Applied Soc. Studies,* 1971.

Ornstein, R. *Psychology of Consciousness.* San Francisco: W. H. Freeman and Co., 1972.

Pearson, A. W. and Davies, G. B. "Leadership Styles and Planning and Monetary Techniques," *R & D Management,* 11, July 1981.

Radcliffe-Brown, A. R. *Structure and Function in Primitive Society.* London: Oxford University Press, 1952.

Schutz, U. C. *FIRO: A Three Dimensional Theory of Interpersonal Behavior.* New York: Rinehart, 1958.

Tuckman, B. W. "Developmental Sequence in Small Groups," *Psych. Bulletin,* 1965.

Wallace, A. F. C. *Culture and Personality* (2nd ed.). New York: Random House, 1970.

MANAGING PROFESSIONALS' MOTIVATIONS: THE CORE GROUP SYSTEM AT BENTON & BOWLES*

Arthur J. Kover

Malott Hall, Cornell University, Ithaca, New York

Theodore F. Dunn

Benton & Bowles

ABSTRACT. Ensuring coordination and cooperation is often a major managerial problem in firms in which there are large numbers of professionals and managers. This problem arises because managers and professionals may be too highly motivated, that is, they tend to substitute individual or departmental goals for the goals of the company. The Core Group enables professionals to have an explicit impact upon the decision-making process. This paper summarizes the use of the Core Group system at Benton and Bowles, a New York advertising agency.

The background

Benton and Bowles is a large New York-based advertising agency. In common with other organizations that utilize large numbers of professionals and managers, this agency was faced with the problem of how to channel highly motivated professionals to assure the maximum amount of cooperation and coordination in the accomplishment of their tasks. This situation was exacerbated by the staffing policies of advertising agencies.

Agencies, in common with other labor-intensive businesses, cannot overstaff to meet frequent overflows in work demand. If they did this, there would be little problem in meeting crises, but then there would be idle and expensive staff waiting for the next crisis to occur. Agencies generally understaff slightly so that normal work demands are met and, if there is a workflow crisis, people either work longer hours or temporary personnel are hired for that crisis.

Because of normal understaffing, service professionals such as creative, research, media, promotion and many junior managers in agencies are assigned to the business of more than one client. This leaves them free (within limits) to select the accounts they "like better" and to pay less attention to those accounts they find less satisfying for some reason. In the absence of a central coordinating system (which would be impossible because of the fluid nature of advertising work), the manager of an agency's account must negotiate or cajole service professionals to devote more time to that account. Even if a service professional person *is* working at full capacity on that piece of business, there is always the likelihood that managers will feel that not enough attention is being given to their accounts. The problem is compounded by the work habits of these professionals. It is a common complaint, and not only in the advertising industry, that coordinating the work of professionals is usually very difficult. This is exactly the opposite of the problems that managers have in motivating line workers; professionals and managers are, if anything, over-motivated. They often become so involved in their own work that getting them to understand, much less work with, professionals with different specialties is often an insurmountable problem. In the advertising industry, in which the only output is the result of different professionals working together with managers to make a custom-made product, this problem is acute.

The top management of Benton and Bowles was aware of this problem; it has bothered the industry for many years. They also knew that other agencies had tried to overcome the situation with varying success [2]. In 1971, the president of the agency announced a new way of transacting some internal business which he called the Core Group system. Beside the basic problem of ensuring adequate participation in all assignments, the president also hoped that this system would help in another area, specifically, that of professionals acting as full members of each group rather than contributing only professional input.

Membership in Core Groups and Core Group meetings

The Core Group idea is a relatively simple one. Managerial personnel assigned to an account belong to a Core Group, as do each of the top level professional people working on that business. Therefore, a person belongs to as many Core Groups as there are accounts to which he or she is assigned. A typical Core Group has six members, as shown in Table 1.

This is not unique. Most advertising agencies have some sort of system of assigning similar people to the work of one or several accounts. What is different is the provision for having these people interact in Core Group meetings.

Core Group meetings can be called by any member. As it turned out, meetings are nearly always called by management people as part of their planning role. During meetings of each Core Group, active member par-

Table 1

Management Supervisor	A senior management person. Generally responsible for over-all guidance of a major portion of the agency's business.
Account Supervisor	The manager responsible for the actual daily running and planning for either one large account or several smaller accounts.
Account Executive	The manager responsible (under the supervision of the account supervisor) for the activities and scheduling of *one* account.
Associate Creative Director	The professional executive responsible for all the "creative work"—copy writing, art and design, and production of advertising—on particular accounts. People under this person's supervision are responsible for executing the actual advertising.
Associate Research Director	The professional executive responsible for advertising and marketing research done by an agency for several accounts.
Associate Media Director	The professional executive responsible for selection, pur-chasing, and placing of advertising in the media for several accounts.

ticipation is encouraged and organizational status barriers are relaxed, to the extent that anyone in the group can talk freely about any aspect of a problem. In fact, the folklore of Core Group meetings is now that almost any opinion (outside of direct insults) can be expressed and there will be no repercussions.

These Core Group meetings are, in a classical sense, *forums* in which planning, communication, and coordination can take place by ensuring participation and making it more attractive to all members of each Core Group.

As described, Core Group meetings were designed to overcome some of the problems of selective participation and of coordination in a "non-managerial" way.

Core Groups were in fact set up to eliminate the "hub" or "leader centered" communication method in which all communications come from or are directed to the account or management supervisor as shown in Figure 1. Instead, a group centered form of communication was encouraged. In a group centered meeting, there is interaction among all members of the group, as is shown in Figure 2.

In addition, the "group centered" meeting helps reduce communication problems arising from serial reproduction. Such problems develop when successive individuals "filter" messages, thereby altering the original meaning by the time they reach the persons for whom they were intended. For example, in the "leader centered" system, when an Associate Creative Director has a problem researched, the problem would often be distorted by the time it was filtered through account management to research.

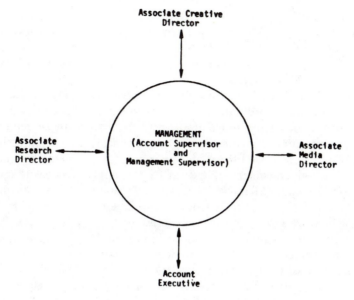

Figure 1. The "HUB" Meeting.

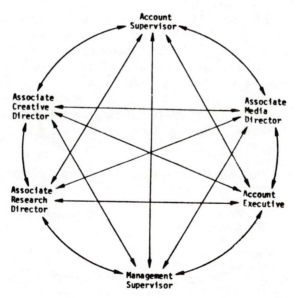

Figure 2. The Group Centered Meeting.

There was little in the nature of coercion in any aspect of Core Group meetings. Rather, they were made attractive as places in which concerned people could interchange information, in which different opinions (even outside of one's specialty) would be respected, and in which members of the Core Group could be a team.

The two objectives of the Core Group system were: (1) service departments would better coordinate their efforts in servicing clients and (2) as a consequence of providing more input, professionals in these departments would derive greater job satisfaction. Benton and Bowles commissioned a study to find out how well these objectives were being met. The study was conducted among members of fifteen of the approximately thirty Core Groups in the agency. All members completed a questionnaire covering their feelings and beliefs about their Core Group meetings as well as their participation in Core Group activities. In addition, management supervisors and two other top management groups completed independent questionnaires. Management supervisors provided self-estimates of their management style. One of the two top management groups evaluated the management supervisors of the 15 Core Groups on their management style. The other group evaluated the client environment within which the Core Groups worked.*

The results
What happens in Core Groups

The Core Group is essentially perceived by members as a means to increase involvement and to open communications. This was precisely one of the objectives of the system. (See Table 2.) It is *not* seen as a team effort or a way to ensure partnership of the members. The idea of team efforts and shared decision making proposed by many in Organizational Development has not taken place here, even though the formal Core Group can allow it. Why?

One reason is that many specialists in these groups do not want to make shared general decisions. They feel more comfortable within the areas in

Table 2. What Are Core Groups? (As Seen By Members).

Means of increasing involvement	44%
Means of opening communications	41%
Way to get input from all concerned people	17%
A cooperative team effort	13%
A partnership of all members	3%
(Multiple responses add to more than 100%)	

* Details of the study can be obtained by writing A. J. Kover.

which they are expert. Further, they do not have the time or the depth of information to want to spend their efforts in decision making.

Finally, the only generalists in these groups are the managers. Their jobs involve overall responsibility for the development of agency marketing and advertising strategies and advertising. In addition, they must communicate and often sell agency recommendations to clients. As such, one of their major responsibilities is to make decisions. If this is lost or abdicated, then the role of management disappears, an event few managers are willing to let happen.

Table 3 shows that members feel Core Group meetings typically are not decision making bodies; instead, they are discussion groups in which members have an opportunity to provide input for decision making. Moreover, they generally discuss policy or strategic issues, not day-to-day short-range problems.

As shown in Table 4, only 14% of the Core Group members said that *nothing* ever gets decided at meetings. Generally, what does get decided by such groups are matters that are either internal or have to do solely with advertising. Issues concerned with new directions or those touching the affairs of clients are less frequently addressed. Put in other words, Core Groups sometimes decide issues which are not too risky.

Thus, the Core Groups in this advertising agency increase involvement and open communications, apparently successfully, among the critical staff and managers on an account. They are primarily discussion groups which make relatively few decisions and ones that are not particularly risky.

How well does the core group system work?

Measuring the effectiveness of a nonline production organization is something like finding out if psychiatric treatment works. When attempts to look at output and productivity fail, the best method is to ask the people involved in the organization itself.

Generally, the people involved in these Core Groups like the idea of the meetings. Although a few middle-level managers thought the meetings a

Table 3. What Kinds of Problems Do Core Groups Generally Work On?

	STRATEGY	TACTICS	TOTAL
Makes decisions	11%	7%	18%
Discuss/provide information	52%	15%	67%
Total	63%	22%	85%

Note: 15% did not answer this question.

Table 4. What Kinds of Things Get Decided?

Material for internal presentation to management	61%
Advertising—general or tactical issues	52%
New advertising directions	42%
Issues of marketing policy (more general than advertising and impinging into the client area)	29%
Nothing gets decided	14%

Note: The figures shown are the ratios of people saying that if an item is discussed, it sometimes is decided in a Core Group. What this table does is hold constant the amount of times something is discussed.

waste of time, most members had positive suggestions to bring the meetings closer to the ideal. Suggested improvements were for more frequent or regularly scheduled meetings, more circulation of information prior to meetings and some sort of formal record of decisions. Even among the grumblers, the level of acceptance of these Core Group meetings was relatively positive. (See Table 5.)

In addition to rating their general attitudes toward the Core Groups, participants rated their Core Group(s) on a large number of specific attributes. The analysis then classified these attributes into four basic dimensions:

—The Core Group is helpful and useful.
—The Core Group is informal and loose.
—The Core Group encourages cooperation and consensus.
—There are lots of fights in this Core Group.

Ratings tended to be better than neutral for these dimensions. The feelings of most of the members were relatively favorable; Core Groups are perceived generally as rather useful, informal, cooperative and without a lot of fights. (See Table 6.)

Table 5. How Should the Core Group System Be Changed or Improved?

Stop it, it doesn't work		11%
Change nothing, it works fine now		18%
Specific Suggested Changes		
More frequent meetings	33%	
More initiative, preparation by members	25%	
Provide more information to members	16%	
(especially staff people)		
—Agendas		
—Written summaries of meetings		
—More information before discussions		
More openness, more integration	10%	
No opinion		15%

Table 6. Attitudes Towards Core Groups Among Members.

		ARE USEFUL AND HELPFUL	ARE INFORMAL	ENCOURAGE COOPERATION AND CONSENSUS	HAVE LOTS OF FIGHTS
Manager's Style					
Core Groups in which the manager is more controlling		0	0	Yes	No
Core Groups in which the Manager is less controlling		0	0	0	Yes
Relations With Client (Environment)					
Core Groups in which relations with clients are placid		0	0	No	0
Core Groups in which relations with clients are unstable		0	0	Yes	0
Manager's Style and Client Relationship					
The manager *is:*	Relations with the client *are:*				
Controlling	Unstable	Yes	Yes	Yes	No
Controlling	Placid	No	No	No	No
Less controlling	Placid	Yes	0	No	Yes
Less controlling	Unstable	No	0	Yes	0

0 = Average level of attitude.

The researchers analyzed answers in different Core Groups in which the top manager's (management supervisor) style differed and in groups which had different kinds of relations with their clients.

Managers' styles were divided into more controlling and less controlling. The more controlling managers reserve more of the decision making to themselves; they see the ultimate responsibility for the success of the Group's operations as being in their hands. Therefore, they tend to want to know everything that goes on (rather than just what they feel they "need to know to make decisions"). They also think that their relations with members of the Core Group are businesslike and brisk. The less controlling managers, on the other hand, consider that the day-to-day decisions are made by members of the Core Group and that their role is to guide, modify, and (when necessary) veto. They feel that they want only the information needed to make higher level decisions; their relations with Core Group members are more close and personal.

Overall, there was little difference in attitudes toward their Core Groups among people belonging to Groups with more controlling and less controlling managers. The top section of Table 6 shows that there is more encouragement of cooperation and consensus when the manager is more controlling and more fights when the manager is less controlling. Perhaps, for groups with controlling managers, the emphasis is on consensus as much as cooperation.

The client-environment was much more complex to measure. Three elements were considered: The tone of the daily dealings between agency and client people; how "secure" that particular piece of business is with clients (the long-range prospects); and the nature of the workload in a group (ranging from easy and predictable to very heavy with crazy deadlines). The groups were classified generally either as relatively placid or relatively unstable.

Again, there is relatively little difference in attitudes toward Core Groups by the degree of placidity or instability. In more unstable groups there is more emphasis on cooperation and less in placid groups. This should not be surprising; appeals to pull together make sense when the going is tough.

Strong differences do emerge when these two kinds of elements are *combined*. A Core Group in an unstable client environment with a controlling manager is perceived as more useful, more informal, more cooperative and with fewer fights. Except for the absence of fights, just the opposite is true of Core Groups in a placid environment with a controlling manager. (See the bottom of Table 6.) For the other two situations, the attitudes are mixed, although Groups are considered more useful when the environment is placid and the manager is less controlling. Thus, although Core Groups are generally perceived favorably by members, there are some sharp differences. Core Groups seem to work best either when the manager is controlling and the environment unstable, or the manager is less controlling and the environment is placid.

This is rather surprising because we might expect that this kind of discussion system would work "best" when the environment is placid and there is time for discussion and/or when the manager is less controlling and the Core Group can take over some of the jobs of management. Then why does this system work well when the manager controls and there are continuous alarms?

The reasons may be these: Core Groups provide information to a manager when the manager needs it; they also can serve as a forum in which differences are aired and resolved so that all Core Group members can present a more unified front to the client.

What can managers learn from the core group experience?

This study of the Core Group system in Benton and Bowles indicates that:

—The Core Group is a forum which provides an opportunity for and encourages interaction among members.

—It breaks down the barriers of formal status relationships.

—It provides rewards by being a platform for recognition of individual contributions.

Core Group members feel that the system:

—Increases their involvement; makes them more totally involved.

—Provides an opening for communications.

—Is desirable; they like it.

—Is a place where they can discuss and provide input for decisions, but don't make the decisions. Those few decisions they do make are more of an advertising than a marketing nature.

Strong differences in members' attitudes about Core Group effectiveness emerge because of different combinations of leadership style and client environment. Core Groups seem to work best when:

—the manager is controlling and the environment is unstable *or*

—the manager is less controlling and the environment is placid.

Going beyond these findings, what are the general principles that come out of this report can help managers manage their (staff professional) people better?

The essential point is that the Core Group system somehow channeled the motivations of different professionals so that they coordinate their activities relatively well. The most obvious reason is that Core Groups funneled motivation by constant challenges, endorsements, discussion, and justification of activities by members. Obviously, this is important but it is not enough. Such challenges, endorsements, and justifications can take place well enough in other environments. Perhaps the key reason is more simple and less obvious.

Some years ago, Chinoy, in his study of automobile factory workers [1], discovered that workers were happier and more productive if they had a more-or-less clear view of the end of the assembly line. If they could *see* the end product of which their work was a part, then they felt that their work meant more. Similar to Chinoy's observation are the feelings of a construction worker who tells a friend, "I helped build *that* building." Many professionals in organizations are akin to line workers; they do not really see the effects of their work nor do they see the end product. Their overmotivation results in part from *wanting* their work to be useful, often in the absence of clear assurance that it is, or if it is, to what degree.

The Core Group provides a frequently used and acceptable arena for fitting one's work into the whole; the professionals can now see the end of the assembly line. At Benton and Bowles, this means that each professional's contribution is fitted *before his or her eyes* into a whole *even if the decision or the actual product is not made by that person*. How much more satisfying to be part of a process that one participates in and sees the direct outcome, than for a person to work hard and then see the final result several months later on television without knowing just what contribution his work actually made.

REFERENCES

[1] Chinoy, Eli, *Automobile Workers and the American Dream,* Boston, Beacon Press, 1965.
[2] Kover, Arthur J. "Reorganization in an Advertising Agency," *Human Organization,* January, 1964.

6
Planning—Control Interaction

Trust in God,
but tie your camel.
Persian Proverb

The next two chapters will discuss operational control of the project. This chapter emphasizes the link between project control and network planning activities. The goal of this chapter is to indicate the relationship between planning and control processes, and to help project managers design control systems that are compatible with the planning process.

A control system should be designed to alert the project manager to potential difficulties so that appropriate remedial action can be taken. A control system is seen as consisting of information, feedback, and action. The chief actors in the control system are the project team members who provide information, feed the information back to the project manager, and participate in necessary action.

A technique useful for information classification is the work breakdown structure. Feedback and action are facilitated by using linear responsibility charting.

PROJECT CONTROL AND CONTROL SYSTEMS

Up to this point, we have been concerned mainly with planning a project. We now turn to a consideration of executing the project plan. The project plan is a projection of future action. Project control involves implementing that projection. The project plan projects inputs and outputs, that is, expenditures and progress towards the final goal. Project control involves the monitoring of the actual expenditure levels and progress to insure that the final goal will be met. Project control systems are procedures that facilitate communication of decisions, expenditures, and progress between team members and the project manager. Since the planning system projects the future and the control system helps to insure that future, the planning and control systems are very much interdependent and need to be built upon similar assumptions.

The first major assumption is that project control, like project planning, is not considered to mean dictating to someone exactly how to perform a certain activity. Project control is not power and manipulation on the part of the project manager or those above him. It is true that the control system necessarily contains information about performance and that project managers could misuse such information if they so desired. Such misuse, however, is what gives control systems their bad name and makes them sound so onerous. In this chapter, the assumed purpose of control systems will be for the sharing of information regarding project expenditures and progress. The use of control systems to maintain someone's power for manipulation is considered to be counterproductive, and team members should work to prevent this from happening.

The objective of a project control system is to provide information such that the project manager can take corrective action. The essential process of control is to monitor progress and expenditures. This needs to be done in such a way that if the project falls behind, the project manager will be alerted in enough time to schedule future corrective action. Although a computer may be used for storing this information, it can only store what the team members provide. This is because most information on expenditures and progress resides with the team members. If they withhold information, either knowingly or unknowingly, the control system will not work, computer or no computer. Thus an essential part of any project control system becomes the existence of free and open communication between team members and the project manager.

The three major elements of a project control system are action, information, and feedback. These elements have a circular relationship, as shown in Figure 6-1. We begin with action, which usually produces information. That is, when an action is taken, the result of that action generates information regarding the effectiveness of that action. This information remains fairly useless for management purposes until it is

Figure 6–1. Elements of Project Control.

organized and presented to the project manager as feedback. Thus feedback is considered to be the process of team members' informing the project manager of the status of the activities on the project. One system often used for organizing the information is called the work breakdown structure, which will be covered in subsequent sections of this chapter.

Since project team members are often new to the project manager and to each other, it is often not clear to them exactly who should be reporting what to the project manager. Responsibility charting will be suggested as a solution to that problem and thus as an integral part of the project control system.

The third element of the control system is remedial action. Three types of remedial action will be considered:

1. *Redesign.* This is necessary when it is found that some of the original activities scheduled for the project are no longer necessary or when new activities are found to be needed. It also occurs when there is a change in final product specification. Redesign of an activity normally means changing some of the original goals of the activity. Redesign of the project would normally require another iteration of the network design process.
2. *Reschedule.* Rescheduling normally requires setting new deadlines for activities and perhaps for the entire project. If you are behind and the task cannot be trimmed, this is often the only feasible solution.
3. *Reallocate.* This involves the reallocation, and usually addition, of assets for future activities. Concepts and methods for reallocation of assets were discussed in Chapter 2.

PROJECT INFORMATION AND FEEDBACK

Many organizations currently have formal information systems which support control of normal company operations. These systems have traditionally been designed to support functional units within the corporate structure. For example, the computerized payroll, accounts receivable, and general ledger systems are designed to help control the corporate finances. Likewise, there are systems for forecasting and tracking sales as well as other functions of the organization. Often there is an attempt to share information among these systems, an effort that goes under the general heading of decision support systems. This is a noble goal and one that is necessary in a project environment. However, for the most part, information systems in today's corporate environment are designed to support decision making according to the traditional organizational structure.

A typical mistake during the design of a project control system is to rely on the organizational information system. Because of the very nature of project management, the project manager must cut across functional organization lines in order to accomplish his goals. Just as the project manager must integrate activities across these departments, he must also be able to integrate information across these departments. Since the systems are designed for the unique needs of each department, there is little chance that similar information is collected in a similar fashion in different departments. Even if different departments are using the same category headings, such as in-process inventory, there is always a chance that they are defining that term in different ways. So the project manager is often faced with the difficult task of coordinating a bewildering array of forms, terms, and reports that require interpretation from one to the next.

Even if the project manager can coordinate various forms, there remains the chance that the information pertinent to a project is not collected anywhere in the corporate information system. Thus it could simply be impossible for the project manager to get the information necessary to run the project from the standard corporate systems.

Another problem with using standard information systems is that reports are often produced long after the actions are taken. A standard quarterly report may not be produced until a month after the quarter is finished. This is often due to the fact that the report is being produced for some outside demand, such as the Internal Revenue Service, and the production schedule for the reports is geared to their timetable. The project manager who wants a report faster better have a friend at the IRS.

Tuman (1983) has summarized some of the more typical problems encountered by project managers trying to do their jobs while relying on existing or traditional management information systems. These are:

1. *Usefulness.* Existing corporate management information systems do not generate the specific information required by the project manager and other project participants. The needed information is not generally available in a useful form, and considerable time and money are required to revise the existing systems to get the data needed in a timely manner.
2. *Quality vs. Quantity.* Too much detailed information is generated. It is necessary to pour through reams of computer printouts to extract the required data. It is difficult to get exception reports, especially when several functions may be involved.
3. *Integration.* There is little uniformity among corporate systems. Hence it is difficult to develop a total picture where several companies are involved. Even within one organization's management information system, it can be very difficult to reconcile information from diverse functions such as finance, personnel, and operations to develop an integrated project status report.
4. *Responsiveness.* Whenever top management requests an answer to a specific question or problem, it initiates a mad scramble to obtain the required data. The existing information systems are not structured to integrate across functions to produce timely exception reports.

So the essence of the difficulty is that many information systems are designed to support each functional area's unique set of problems. Those problems are not necessarily the problems of the project manager. This is now a fairly well-recognized fact. What is usually needed is a project information and control system specifically suited to the unique needs of project management.

The most important element of a project information system is people, particularly the people who are performing the activities. With a good working relationship and a climate of trust, people will usually be ready to share the information they possess. This is particularly true when the information concerns a project they helped to design and when the sharing is done to assist other members of a team of which they are a part.

This being the case, the interaction between planning and control becomes clearer. Participation in the planning of the project makes the need for a control system more obvious. It also helps people to determine the parts needed to make up the control system, such as who will report what information to whom. The project team members thus become important participants in the design and success of the project information system.

Yet however eager the project team members may be to share information, the reporting responsibilities, relationships, and formats are anything but clear when the project begins. Some sort of structure is usually needed in order to facilitate communication. With this in mind, we turn to a consideration of information system structure.

PROJECT INFORMATION SYSTEM STRUCTURE

The elements of the information system structure include the network and bar charts designed during the project planning phase, a work breakdown structure (WBS) used to classify cost elements, and a linear responsibility chart (LRC) used to specify responsibilities in the project team.

The design of the network and bar charts has been covered in detail in Chapters 3 and 4. A WBS is a graphic picture of the hierarchy of the project broken down by level into subprojects and finally into activities. This diagram is expressed in detail from the top down in a tree structure. A WBS establishes the way in which cost and schedule data will be tracked and reported. A linear responsibility chart replaces the standard organizational chart. This new chart identifies specific management responsibilities with various activities or groups of activities. The combination of the network charts, the WBS, and the LRC facilitates the proper summarization of cost and schedule status to provide a measure of project progress.

Fundamental to the integration of the network charts, the linear responsibility chart, and the work breakdown structure are cost tracking by activity and the reporting of cost based on the schedule of planned work. It is felt that accurate status of the project can be determined by knowing the cost and time of completed activities and then comparing these figures with the remaining time and budget. These comparisons yield cost and time estimates to complete the project. The information system is integrated when cost and time for each activity are reported using the WBS code. The LRC indicates the person responsible for the activities that are being examined. Examples of both of these concepts are reviewed below.

WORK BREAKDOWN STRUCTURE (WBS)

The WBS is essentially a coding scheme that assigns meaningful numbers as codes for the various elements of the work to be done on a project. The coding scheme is based on a hierarchy of task relationships. By utilizing the WBS code to structure information transfer, communication can be simplified. This happens when all communication and reporting of expenditures for the project is done using the common code. If properly implemented, the WBS can become the common language of the project. It works well as a device whereby diverse users can communicate back and forth from the very inception of the project to its completion.

The use of a WBS for project control proceeds in three phases:

1. Construction of the code along with responsibilities and budgets
2. Reporting of expenditures and progress
3. Reconciliation against time and budgets

Construction of Code, Responsibilities, and Budgets

The WBS can normally be derived from the network chart devised for the project. In reality, the network and the WBS are constructed at the same time. The original group that prepares the outline and the concept of the project defines it to a stage from which the WBS can be prepared. Normally, the activities will fall into logical groupings. For example, certain activities will all be done by the engineering department, while others will be done by the plant department. The coding system is used to assign numbers to the elements in this logical grouping.

Consider as an example a project to build and start up a new facility at a new location. Suppose further that the project manager has determined that this entire project logically falls into four groupings, which we will call subprojects. The four subprojects are (1) overall design, (2) layout design, (3) installation, and (4) testing. These four subprojects will be the responsibility of four departments in the organization: (1) engineering, (2) plant, (3) construction, and (4) operations. People from these departments form a project team and produce a network chart for the project. During this process, they define the activities to be completed. Some activities are large and are broken down into subactivities. From the outcome of this process, the WBS for the project is derived, as shown in Figure 6–2.

Many projects are similar to this example in that they contain a natural hierarchy of both tasks and responsibilities. The top of the hierarchy is the entire project, with the project manager responsible. The next level down is represented by the departments, with each department head assumed to be responsible for all activities performed in that department. The third level involves the actual activities in which someone from each department would be responsible.

PROJECT BREAKDOWN	DESCRIPTION	WBS CODE
Project	New facility	1000
Subproject 1	Overall design	1100
Activity 1	Location analysis	1110
Activity 2	Choose design	1120
Subproject 2	Layout design	1200
Activity 1	Machine layout	1210
Activity 2	Work flow design	1220
Subproject 3	Installation	1300
Activity 1	Fabrication	1310
Activity 2	Setup	1320
Subactivity 1	Ship parts to site	1321
Subactivity 2	Assemble parts	1322
Subactivity 3	Test building	1323
Activity 3	Install equipment	1330
Subproject 4	Testing	1400
Activity 1	Test equipment	1410
Activity 2	Produce sample product	1420

Figure 6–2. WBS Example.

Finally, some activities may be subdivided, with still other people from the departments given responsibility.

Since there are four groupings in this example, the WBS code consists of four digits. The first digit represents the project number. The second digit represents a code for each department. The third digit is a code for each activity, and the fourth digit is a code for any sub-activities.

The WBS code is designed such that an entry at any level is the summation of all entries at the next lower level (see Figure 6–2). Each digit in the code, starting from the left, represents a different level. For example, consider the first level is the entire project. The first digit in the WBS represents this first level. The second digit represents the sub-projects that split up the original project into smaller parts. The entire project is thus said to be a summation of all the subproject entries. These are the entries that have the same first digit as the project code and a different second digit, representing the subproject code, with the last two digits as zeros.

Similarly, subprojects represent the summation of all entries with the same second digit of the WBS code, a different third digit, and the last digit as zero. For example, subproject 2, layout design, is the summation of all entries that have the digit 2 in the second position of their WBS code and a different digit in the third position. Thus subproject 2, with code 1200, consists of machine layout (1210) and work flow design (1220).

While the code is being developed, responsibilities and budgets can also be developed and structured using the same code numbers. In this way, reporting and accounting relationships can be discussed and understood by means of the same WBS codes that are used for the activities.

In terms of authority, the first digit represents the most responsible person, the project manager. The second digit in the example represents the people in charge of the various departments. The third and fourth digits represent people in the various departments that are carrying out the activities or subactivities. The position in the code does not necessarily represent the amount of responsibility, but it does indicate the level of responsibility. Thus a person at level two may not be responsible for overseeing the actual work done by a person at level three but may be responsible for the overall quality of that work. An example of this coding is shown in Figure 6–3.

WBS CODE	BUDGET (000)	RESPONSIBILITY
1000	5,000	Phil Pidcock, PM
1100	1,000	Engineering Dept.
1110	500	Tom Guilemore
1120	500	Dennis Cohand
1200	1,000	Plant Dept.
1210	700	Bert Cohand
1220	300	Tom Berned
1300	2,000	Construction Dept.
1310	500	Larry Hishorn
1320	1200	Patty Padrizi
1321	500	Joe Doaks
1322	500	Jim Doaks
1323	200	John Doaks
1330	300	Gym Cranz
1400	1,000	Operations Dept.
1410	600	Roz Lawn
1420	400	Debby Grimes

Figure 6-3. WBS Coding for Budgets and Responsibility.

In terms of budgeting, the same relationship holds. That is, the budget amount for the first level is the budget for the entire project. The subprojects are assigned a portion of this total amount, and the sum of the budgets of all subprojects equals the budget amount for the entire project. The breakdown continues through the activities and subactivities. An example of this is shown in Figure 6-3.

Reporting of Expenditures and Progress

The operational use of WBS is for reporting expenditures and progress. Some organizations use two separate but related systems for keeping track of expenditures and progress: a project accounting system and a project control system (Lavold, 1983). A project accounting system is often created to handle expenses, while the project control system concentrates on progress. The project accounting and project control systems will both collect data using the WBS. These systems receive data on the common basis of the dictionary and code structure directly associated with the WBS.

The project control systems, whether manual or automated, collect timely information which is current and which can be used for management reporting and decision making. The importance of the project control system is its early warning capability. These systems do not have precise cost information but supply vital current information needed to control the project. All information is collected, sorted, and reported via the WBS code structure. The project control systems use this code for all aspects of monitoring cost, schedule, and productivity and for future planning.

The project accounting systems, which by design are precise but not normally as timely as the project control systems, collect the official or auditable information for cost or resource usage on the project. This information is collected, for example, from invoices from contractors, time sheets from personnel working on the project, and expenses of the personnel doing the work. This information can be coded using WBS, with payments being recorded for the WBS elements. Having the project accounting system able to verify the actual costs that were spent against the estimate and against the budget by common means allows the actual cost of the progress to date to be tracked against the estimate of cost as well as against the forecast.

Reconciliation against Time and Budget

One of the problems typically present in many projects is that the accounting and project control systems are not using identical coding. By utilizing the WBS in conjunction with the existing accounting coding system this problem can be somewhat alleviated. As a project proceeds, upper management may call for an explanation of the differences between what was budgeted and what has actually been spent. The way to provide this information is anything but clear, as the reasons for differences are often subtle and complex. However, if the project control and the project accounting systems are using two different coding schemes, the project manager may find the task close to impossible. If they are both using the WBS codes, it is much easier to reconcile the differences. Thus, the key to providing proper explanations is the disciplined usage of WBS coding by every person involved in both systems.

PROJECT FEEDBACK AND ACTION

A project control system was previously said to consist of information, feedback, and action. Up to this point, we have mainly been concerned with classifying and coding information. A WBS was described as a useful tool to aid in the collection and transmitting of information on project progress and expenditures. Such a coding scheme, however, does not tell us what information is to be relayed to whom, and what types of actions that person is expected to take.

From the WBS responsibility list, we know who is ultimately responsible for each activity, subproject, and project. However, as we know from the network charting exercises, all of these activities and most of the subprojects are interrelated. Changes and delays in one activity may affect several other activities. Thus, though each person has responsibility for his own activity, he is also responsible for giving information to others that may affect the other person's activity. Though most people will agree with such statements, the responsibility of who gives what to whom, and what decisions can or should be made is usually anything but clear.

Linear responsibility charting (LRC) is a management technique designed to help make responsibilities clear in an organization. In most organizations, a person's primary responsibility is usually clear. This responsibility is given in the job title or the job description. What is usually not clear is the support area. That is, who is the person supposed to support and who is supposed to support him? Support responsibilities are often assumed but less often stated. One finds out support relationships by being in the job for a while.

Learning your set of primary and supporting responsibilities is often called learning your role in the organization. Learning one's role often takes a great deal of time and a great deal of practice. Cleland (1982) offers the following analogy for thinking about role definition:

> If a manager were to coach a football team he would doubtlessly take great care to define the role of each player. After a player's role was defined, then the coach would work with the team to develop supportive roles among the players to facilitate the group strategy necessary to win. The roles would be built around specific "territories" that each player would cover. . . . Practice would be required until the degree of understanding and commitment necessary to develop a winning team existed.
>
> No coach would think of putting a football team on the field of play without definition and much practice.

Responsibility charting is a way of systematically clarifying relationships among team members (Gilmore, 1979). The development of team cohesion is greatly facilitated if the individual and collective roles on the team are properly understood. Delineating and keeping faithful to areas of responsibility help also to build trust among the team members.

Responsibility charting should definitely be used as the team is beginning to execute the initial project plan. It can also be used again any time during the project when there seem to be communications difficulties or when aspects of the plan are not being done because of mistaken responsibilities.

RESPONSIBILITY CHARTING PROCESS

Introduction.   Responsibility charting is a way of systematically clarifying relationships among

1. Decisions
2. Actors
3. Types of participation of each actor in each decision

About all that is needed is a blank piece of paper and a willingness to discuss roles and responsibilities. The process is outlined here.

STEP 1: Make a Decision Matrix Form
Down the left side of the blank paper, list the decisions that are at issue. They may be decisions which are made periodically in the organization during everyday operations, proposed decisions for a new project, etc. The choice depends upon the purpose of the group meeting. Across the top, list the actual and/or potential actors who are relevant to the listed decisions regardless of whether they are in or out of the organization.

STEP 2: Develop Mutually Understood Codes
           to Describe Type of Participation
The codes to be used should be home grown, in a language natural to the culture of the organization. They must be rich enough to capture significant differences. A starting set of terms is:

A = *approve*—a person who must sign off or veto a decision before it is implemented or must select from options developed by the R role; accountable for the quality of the decision.

R = *responsible*—the person who takes the initiative in the particular area, develops the alternatives, analyzes the situation, makes the initial recommendation, and is accountable if nothing happens in the area.

C = *consulted*—a person who must be consulted prior to a decision being reached, but with no veto power.

I = *informed*—a person who must be notified after a decision but before it is publicly announced; someone who needs to know the outcome for other related tasks but need not give input.

DK = *don't know*.

A blank indicates no relationship.

A useful way of testing the understanding of the codes is to have each project team member describe a recent decision by means of these terms; then compare to see if all are interpreting them in a similar fashion. Often groups modify these basic terms with subscripts or by using capitals and lower case or adding new terms. Prior to balloting (STEP 3), it is important for participants to be using the terms in similar ways.

STEP 3: Individual Balloting on the Decisions
Give each participant a copy of the decision matrix and key definitions of the types of participation. Working horizontally, each respondent should fill out the chart as he or she thinks that decision *is* made, not how it should be made or how it is prescribed in some manual. People should fill out all columns, not just their own.

STEP 4: Record the Data
Collect the forms and record the aggregate results on a large form that can be seen by the whole group or on a smaller form, with copies distributed to the group. Ideally, this recording should be done after

the first meeting, with a later meeting scheduled for analysis and discussion. A useful technique is to record the data on overhead transparencies to help in the negotiation.

STEP 5: Analyze and Discuss the Data
There are three major aspects to the analysis. The first involves clarification of discrepancies in how different parties see decisions being made. The second and third involve discussions about the overall pattern across roles (horizontal) or across decisions (vertical).

A. *Analysis of Discrepancies*
  If a large number of discrepancies exist between the codes entered by the decision maker for him- or herself and those entered by others, the group needs to clarify what is going on. Often the process of responsibility charting itself will help to improve this condition.

Possible Discrepancies

YOU SEE YOUR ROLE AS	OTHERS SEE IT AS	CONSEQUENCE
A	R	You are waiting to make final sign-off type decision and looking to others to develop the alternatives. They are looking to you for the major initiative. Possible lack of action in this area, with you blaming others for not delivering while they in turn are looking to you.
R	A	You want the central role, developing the alternatives; others see you as a final sign-off and perhaps give you too little information and involve you later than you want in the decision process.
C	I	You want a chance to make substantive input before the decision. Others see you as only needing to be informed.
I	C	You want to know the decision, but not be involved. Others will draw on your time expecting input when you don't feel the need for involvement. Problems arise when others wait for your response while you feel you are only being informed.

Once people have worked through to a shared understanding of the allocation of responsibility, they can turn to the overall patterns.

B. *Vertical Analysis by Decision Maker*

FINDING	POSSIBLE INTERPRETATION OR QUESTION
1. Lots of R's	Can or need the individual stay on top of so much?
2. No empty spaces	Does the person need to be involved in so many decisions, or could management by exception principles be used, perhaps reducing C's to I's or leaving it to the individual's discretion when something needs particular attention?
3. No R's or A's	If a line position, it may be a weak role that could either be enlarged or eliminated.
4. Overall pattern as against the personality type of the role occupant	Does the pattern fit the personality and style of the role occupant—too little involvement, too much, etc.

C. *Horizontal Analysis by Decisions*

1. No R's	Job may not get done; everyone waiting to approve, be consulted, or be informed; no one sees his role to take the initiative.
2. Lots of A's	Diminished accountability. With so many people signing off, it may be too easy to shift the blame around.
3. Lots of C's	Do all these individuals really need to be consulted? Have the costs of consulting in terms of delay and communication time been weighed against the benefits of more input?
4. Lots of I's	Do all these individuals need to be routinely informed, or could they be informed only in exceptional circumstances?

Advantages and Uses of Responsibility Charting

Focus on Tasks. Responsibility charting focuses on tasks instead of raising sensitive interpersonal issues. It does not require third-party facilitation. It values multiple perspectives and sharpens the group's understanding of its differences prior to resolving them. It is data based and moves from specifics to general policies, much like case law. Finally, it acknowledges the true complexity of organizations as opposed to tables of organization that hide as much as they reveal.

Conflict Resolution. On a project team in which role confusion exists, responsibility charting can be a powerful diagnostic tool that clearly surfaces the different perceptions of the existing situation and enables problem solving bargaining to take place around the design of a new arrangement. Rather than fighting win/lose battles on a specific decision between two actors, responsibility charting allows trade-offs among a richer set of decisions, among a larger group of actors, and with a subtler classification of the types of involvement in various decisions. It is particularly powerful in low communication/low contact situations (e.g., central office, field office) because it develops a substantial amount of data on the perceptions in which intragroup variability is likely to exist and establishes a point of overlap before issues become polarized. Again, anonymity prevents enforcing of group loyalty.

Training. Responsibility charting is useful in training contexts to generate substantive discussions that will help individuals understand who is involved in what decisions and how they interrelate. In a short time, a wide range of decisions can be discussed that would otherwise require several months of experience. It can clarify in advance sensitive issues of sanctioning of employees, promotions, and layoffs, as well as identify under what conditions people should involve others (management by exception). At one extreme, it could be used systematically to brief a new employee on his relationship not only to the immediate supervisor, but also to other units and other levels.

Job Analysis. Responsibility charting can be used to examine the decisional subset of specific jobs to raise questions about overload, underload, or fit with the role occupant.

Accountability. Responsibility charting can enhance accountability by clearly identifying in advance the expectations as to how various actors will relate to key decisions: who will be blamed for errors of omission (e.g., nothing is done—no one sees role as R) and errors of commission (A is perhaps ultimately and publicly responsible, but will hold R internally accountable for that role).

SUMMARY

This chapter has concentrated on the interaction between the planning and the control functions of project management. It was argued that the complete project manager is aware that the control system should be planned for the project. This means that the organizational control system should not be adopted uncritically. The complete project manager also realizes that the purpose of control is for scheduling remedial action. The complete project manager communicates the idea to the project team in both word and deed. The complete project manager structures the information for the control system along project lines using a work breakdown structure. The complete project manager also assigns responsibility for project actions using responsibility charting.

REFERENCES

Charette, W. and Halverson, W. "Tools of Project Management" in *The Implementation of Project Management: The Professional's Handbook* (L. Stuckenbruck, ed.). Reading, Mass.: Addison Wesley, 1981.

Cleland, D. "The Professional in Matrix Management," *Proceedings of the Project Management Institute Annual Seminar/Symposium,* 1982.

Gilmore, T. "Managing Collaborative Relationships in Complex Organizations," *Administration of Social Work,* 3(2), 1979.

Lavold, G. "Developing and Using the Work Breakdown Structure" in *Project Management Handbook,* (D. Cleland and W. King, Eds.). New York: Van Nostrand Reinhold, 1983.

McCann, J. and Gilmore, T. "Diagnosing Organizational Decision Making through Responsibility Charting," *Sloan Management Review, 24*(2), Winter 1983.

Tuman, J., Jr. "Development and Implementation of Effective Project Management Information and Control Systems" in *Project Management Handbook* (D. Cleland and W. King, Eds.). New York: Van Nostrand Reinhold, 1983.

TOWARD A PSYCHOLOGICAL THEORY OF ACCOUNTABILITY*

Stephen Knouse

Behrend College, The Pennsylvania State University, Erie, Pennsylvania

Accountability is becoming an increasingly significant concept in the management literature. The traditional association of accountability with budgetary control and hence an economic perspective has been expanded to include responsibility for the worth of the individual as advocated in human resource accounting [14]. The demand for accountable performance has also increased [16]. Although the term accountability is becoming more visible,

*Copyright © 1979, *Interfaces* 9(3), pp. 58–63. The Institute of Management Sciences, 290 Westminster Street, Providence, Rhode Island 02903.

there has been relatively little work done in understanding the psychological processes involved. Two questions arise. First, what establishes accountability? Second, what motivates accountable behavior? This paper attempts to provide a basic groundwork for answering these questions.

A definition of accountability

Webster's Third International Dictionary [19] variously defines accountability as: (1) the state of being accountable (answerable or explainable), (2) the state of being liable, and (3) the state of being responsible (p. 13). For our purposes, the definitions of "liable" and "responsible" are relevant.

"Held liable" captures the way many of us think of accountability. If something under your jurisdiction goes wrong, you expect repercussions. This gives a negative flavor to accountability. The latter definition of responsibility, however, provides more meaning and a more positive tone. Responsibility implies feelings of duty, reliability, trust, and importance. In fact, one of the definitions of responsibility is "moral and mental accountability" [19, p. 1935]. Thus I believe accountability should be linked to personal perceptions of responsibility and interwoven with a personal value system. I will develop these ideas further in a model of accountability. But first the traditional organizational views should be explored.

Traditional views of accountability

Several management theorists present various approaches to accountability. Koontz and O'Donnell [11] believe that accountability obliges the subordinate to do all assigned and implied duties. They equate accountability with responsibility arising from the superior-subordinate relationship. Accountability results from a contractual agreement in which the subordinate performs services in return for certain rewards. Hicks and Gullett [5] state that accountability is a commodity that the individual exchanges for the authority to perform given duties. Flippo and Munsinger [4] agree that accountability is a derivative of authority. If you are delegated enough authority to fulfill the responsibilities of the position, accountability is established.

The views of educational administration literature offer an additional perspective. Basically, educators see accountability as a set of procedures leading to the desired end of better instruction. The sequence of events begins with a set of performance standards mutually agreed upon by the teacher and superior. This start is followed by teaching performance attempting to meet these standards. The final step in the sequence is feedback about how well standards were actually met [17].

To summarize, the management and educational literature present several important views of accountability. Accountability is viewed as a responsibility, an obligation, a commodity in an exchange relationship, and a set of procedures leading to better performance. From a psychological viewpoint, a number of characteristics of the accountability relationship are indicated. There is the notion of accountability as social control in addition to economic control of the individual. In other words, you feel accountable because of interpersonal influences as well as because you desire the rewards implied in the accountability agreement. In addition, participation in goal setting, commitment to these goals, and performance monitoring are also important.

Two models of accountability

Recent thought has tended to stress various psychological processes underlying accountability, particularly social control mechanisms. I would like to focus upon two models which differ in orientation but provide bases for understanding the structure of accountability and the motivation for accountable performance (see Table 1).

Table 1. Two models of accountability.

| | MODEL | |
COMPONENTS OF ACCOUNTABILITY	LAWLER-RHODE ORGANIZATIONAL CONTROL MODEL	KNOUSE INDIVIDUAL MODEL
Structure		
Criteria for measuring accountable behavior	Performance Standards	Performance Expectations
Evidence of accountable behavior	Sensor Information	Performance Meeting Expectations
Assessor of accountable behavior	Discriminator	Constituency
Motivation		
The direction and maintenance of accountable behavior	External Motivation (rewards, punishments)	Compliance with Constituency to Receive Rewards
	Internal Motivation (work itself)	Identification with Constituency
		Internalization of Expectations

Lawler and Rhode [13] approach the situation from an organizational perspective. Theirs is a general control model of organizational behavior that operates much like a thermostat. First, there must be a set of performance standards mutually agreed upon by the individual and his or her superiors for establishing accountability. Second, there must be a sensor providing information on how well the individual meets these standards. The sensor might be a set of production statistics or the verbal report of an individual assessing performance. Third, there must be a discriminator, such as one's superiors or perhaps one's work group, who compares sensor information to performance standards and judges whether the standards were met.

Finally, there must be some motivation for the individual to strive to meet the standards of performance (analogous to some type of energy driving the thermostat). Lawler and Rhode identify two categories of motivation. External motivation refers to rewards and punishments dispensed by the organization for meeting standards. Internal motivation, on the other hand, involves those satisfactions the individual gets from the work itself—the variety of tasks performed, successful completion of the work, and the responsibility for scheduling tasks.

Lawler and Rhode [13] offer several characteristics of a successful control system based upon their model. First, participation of the individual in setting standards is important, as such participation strengthens commitment to these standards. Second, a discriminator with more experience has a positive influence on the accountability of the person being measured. A superior performing his or her job well can provide guidance to the individual and thus enhance successful performance. Further, a superior who uses the sensor information well (evaluates the individual accurately and fairly) provides better feedback as to how well standards were met. Third, the motivation to be accountable combines both external organizational rewards and internal rewards of work satisfaction.

I have proposed a model of accountability that focuses more on the individual within society [10]. According to my model, the basis for establishing accountable performance lies in psychological role theory. Katz and Kahn [6] define role as a set of expected behaviors which constitute a position within an organization. Roles are defined by the role-sending process, which is simply the group telling the individual what is expected; he or she then exhibits appropriate behaviors, and receives feedback on how well performance met expectations. The role-sending process is similar to the accountability procedures of the educational literature previously mentioned.

For this model, the criteria for measuring accountability are the role expectations you receive from your constituency (superiors and peers in the work group). The measure of accountability is then how well your behavior meets these expectations. The assessor who determines how well expectations are met we call the individual's constituency.

The motivational components of the model have been borrowed from Kelman's theory of social influence processes [7]. Basically, Kelman states that the individual is motivated to adhere to the desires of one's group because of one of three methods of influence—compliance, identification, or internalization. Compliance produces adherence because the individual desires some reward controlled by the group (e.g., pay or promotion). Compliance is similar to Koontz and O'Donnell's accountability contract where one performs in return for rewards dispensed by the organization. Because the dispensing of rewards depends on appropriate behavior, constant surveillance (observation) of the individual by the group is required to insure accountability by compliance. The organizational psychology research literature has shown that accountability in terms of surveillance is effective, particularly if the group is cohesive and the individual's status is conferred by the group [2], [8], [9].

Identification is a more pervasive means of influence because the individual adheres to the group's desires in order to maintain his or her relationship with the group. In other words, the individual at least partially defines his or her self in terms of the group. Identification as a means of enhancing accountability might then be strengthened through emulation of strong leader figures in the group [6], interests and goals shared among group members [7], and recognition and status that the individual gains from belonging to the group [18].

Internalization is the most powerful means of influence. Here the individual embeds the group's expectations within his or her own value system. The expectations thus become the individual's own goals. Accountability is enhanced therefore if the individual internalizes the expectations of performance—the criteria of performance. Internalization occurs if the individual accepts the expectations because he or she is trying to do the right thing [1]. The perceived expertise (credibility) of the constituency in formulating and sending expectations has been proposed as increasing the rightness the individual associates with the expectations [1]. Further, participation of the individual in arriving at expectations produces internalization by creating a sense of ownership of the expectations [15].

Table 1 demonstrates several similarities between the Lawler and Rhode model and my proposed model. Their performance standards as the criteria for accountability correspond to expectations of performance. In terms of the assessor of accountable performance, their discriminator translates to the constituency of the present model. The major divergence between the two models is in the means of motivating accountable behavior. Lawler and Rhode focus upon an internal-external dichotomy contrasting the work itself (internal motivation) with the consequences meted out by the organization for performance of that work (external motivation). The model I propose, on the other hand, centers upon the social influences in the work setting.

The internal-external duality of the Lawler-Rhode model has aroused much interest in the motivational literature [3], [12]. It is my contention, however, that a social influence approach, such as I have employed, provides a broader framework for understanding the motivational processes of accountability. There are definitely areas of overlap between the models. The concept of compliance (performing to receive desired rewards) equates with Lawler and Rhode's external motivation. Further, the ideas of ownership of expectations and internal reward run common to both Lawler and Rhode's internal motivation [13] and Kelman's internalization [1], [7]. The social influence approach, however, also addresses the interpersonal environment of the individual (i.e., the role relationships with superiors and peers) in which accountability is set.

I originally posed two questions. First, what establishes accountability? The answer appears to be the acceptance of role expectations sent by one's superiors and coworkers. Second, what motivates accountable behavior? The social influence processes of compliance, identification, and internalization serve to produce and maintain behaviors directed toward meeting performance expectations.

Conclusions

Accountability has been examined in traditional terms and in more recent terms of organizational control and role theory. The traditional approach has focused upon accountability as the state of being held liable for one's performance. It is proposed that the concept of accountability be expanded to include processes of social control as well as the rewards and punishments meted out in the traditional accountability setting. If accountability is redefined according to the performance expectations in the work environment, social influence processes leading to compliance, identification, and internalization of role expectations should then strengthen one's motivation to be accountable.

Implications for management

Framed within the processes outlined here, we propose the following guidelines to increase accountability:

1. *Make it crystal clear who is accountable to whom.*

The delineation of clear, direct accountability relationships allows the individual to know exactly what the work group (peers and supervisors) desires. Unambiguous role expectations, which comprise the structure of accountability, are thus easy to deduce.

2. *Involve the individuals in setting levels of their performance for accountability.*

Participation imparts a sense of ownership of accountability standards [15] and hence increases the internal acceptance of accountability.

3. *Tie accountability to how the work is done as well as results.*

Several advantages exist for linking accountability to the behaviors contributing to work performance as well as the results of such performance. According to Lawler and Rhode [13], the individual usually possesses a greater feeling of responsibility over his or her immediate behaviors in a work situation and hence can more easily accept expectations for these specific actions. In addition, assessing accountability for *how* work is approached requires more interaction with the individual and thus more feedback concerning accomplishments. Further, such frequent feedback generates a greater probability of successfully producing the end result for which the individual is ultimately accountable.

4. *Tie accountability to work relationships as well as outcomes.*

Evaluating accountability in terms of successful interpersonal efforts places emphasis upon cooperation, support, and feedback with peers and supervisors. Such group interaction strengthens the identification aspect of accountability.

5. *Enhance the credibility of those who assess accountability (one's constituency).*

The credibility of the people evaluating you has been indicated as one factor which increases the acceptance of performance expectations [1], [7]. This credibility is reflected in the effectiveness of evaluations of accountable behavior. Enlarging the number of peers and supervisors assessing the individual produces a broader perspective for such evaluation. Increasing the frequency of observation of the individual results in more data available for a more accurate assessment of accountability.

In sum, a social control framework for accountability implies that management should look to techniques enhancing self-control, internal commitment, and interpersonal influence. I argue that these methods will strengthen basic perceptions *and acceptance* of accountability.

REFERENCES

[1] Aronson, E., *The Social Animal* (2nd ed.), Freeman, San Francisco, 1976.
[2] Breaugh, J. A. and Klimoski, R. J., The Choice of a Group Spokesman in Bargaining: Member or Outsider? *Organizational Behavior and Human Performance,* Vol. 19, 1977, 325–336.
[3] Deci, E. L., *Intrinsic Motivation,* Plenum, New York, 1975.
[4] Flippo, E. B. and Munsinger, G. M. *Management* (3rd ed.), Allyn and Bacon, Boston, 1975.

[5]   Hicks, H. G. and Gullet, C. R., *Organizations: Theory and Behavior,* McGraw-Hill, New York, 1975.

[6]   Katz, D. and Kahn, R. L., *The Social Psychology of Organizations,* Wiley, New York, 1966.

[7]   Kelman, H. C., Three Processes of Social Influence, *Public Opinion Quarterly,* Vol. 25, 1961, 57–78.

[8]   Klimoski, R. J., The Effects of Intragroup Forces on Intergroup Conflict Resolution, *Organizational Behavior and Human Performance,* Vol. 8, 1972, 363–383.

[9]   ———, and Ash, R. A., Accountability and Negotiator Behavior, *Organizational Behavior and Human Performance,* Vol. 11, 1974, 409–425.

[10] Knouse, S. B., An Analysis of the Processes of Accountability in Negotiating Behavior (doctoral dissertation, The Ohio State University, 1977), *Dissertation Abstracts International,* Vol. 38, 1977, 2412B (University Microfilms No. 77-24,651).

[11] Koontz, H. and O'Donnell, C., *Principles of Management* (5th ed.), McGraw-Hill, New York, 1972.

[12] Lawler, E. E., *Motivation in Work Organizations,* Brooks/Cole, Monterey, Cal., 1973.

[13] ———, and Rhode, J. G., *Information and Control in Organizations,* Goodyear, Pacific Palisades, Cal., 1976.

[14] Likert, R. and Bowers, D. G., Organizational Theory and Human Resources Accounting, *American Psychologist,* Vol. 24, 1969, 585–592.

[15] Lowin, A., Participative Decision-Making: A Model, Literature Critique, and Prescriptions for Research, *Organizational Behavior and Human Performance,* Vol. 3, 1968, 68–106.

[16] Measuring How Well Ads Sell, *Business Week,* September 13, 1976, pp. 104–108.

[17] Pino, E. C., An Operational Accountability Model, in *Accountability: A State, a Process, or a Product,* W. J. Gephart (ed.), Phi Delta Kappa, Bloomington, Ind., 1975.

[18] Shaw, M. E., *Group Dynamics: The Psychology of Small Group Behavior* (2nd ed.), McGraw-Hill, New York, 1976.

[19] *Webster's Third New Unabridged International Dictionary,* Miriam, Springfield, Mass., 1970.

7
People—Control Interaction

*It is only the first bottle
that is expensive.*
French Proverb

This chapter is concerned with human reactions to standards and controls. The purpose of the chapter is to enable the project manager to understand what team members might be thinking, feeling, and subsequently, doing as the project progresses and they come in contact with the project control system.

The first part of the answer lies in the technical nature of the control system itself. Another part lies in team members' perceptions of control and control systems. These perceptions are partly due to the individuals and partly due to the actions of the project manager. Much of the team members' reaction depends on what the project manager does with the control information. Also, as the introductory proverb indicates, perceptions can change over time. Thus, this chapter concentrates on perceptions and reactions.

PEOPLE AND CONTROL

The essential element for successful project control is not so much the sophistication of the control system as it is the interaction of the team members with the control system. This includes not only the interaction of the team members with the formal control system but also the way in which the project manager envisions and uses control. Project managers have a definite need to know how the project is progressing, but they sometimes forget that team members would also like to know this. In addition, the project manager is usually in a position of having to answer to members of top management when they ask how things are going. With this type of pressure, the project manager may feel that he or she must know every detail about every activity. This could result in constantly asking for detailed information about progress. As a result of the constant surveillance, control systems are often perceived as onerous, and people begin to feel overcontrolled and spied upon. For these and other reasons which will be reviewed, most people have a negative perception and subsequent reaction to control systems.

In this book, the assumption is that control is being used to monitor progress against the schedule. When an activity falls behind schedule, and the activity has not been changed since the time it was scheduled, the project manager can make one of several assumptions concerning the cause of the delay. Some of the possible assumptions are:

1. Activity time was underestimated.
2. The people doing the activity are not working hard enough.
3. The environment changed.

Considering the first assumption, we know that activity times are often underestimated. Many times, the original estimate was just a guess. This being the case, the only logical solution is to reschedule. However, many people do not like to reschedule since it reveals that they were not correct in the first place. So even if rescheduling is the logical solution, the project manager might be tempted to prod the employees to work harder in hopes that they can make up for the poor estimate.

When we consider the second assumption, such a conclusion seems to indicate a lack of trust on the part of the project manager. For the trusting manager, there are alternative explanations and actions for what seems to be slow work. For one, it may just seem that the team is behind as it may be working on the "term paper" model discussed in Chapter 2. If this is the case, the manager should probably do nothing. However, if trust is missing, the manager may assume that people are not working hard enough. In this case, the manager might be tempted to prod the employees to work harder.

Note that in either case, the management action is similar, to prod the employees to work harder. Now look from the point of view of the employees. For the manager to know that things are behind, the team members probably gave him the necessary information. As a result of producing the information, the answer they receive is to work harder. This may be interpreted by the project team as a lack of trust, even if the first assumption of poor time estimating was used by the manager. That is, the team members may not know which assumption was used by management, so they will probably assume the worst—that they are not trusted.

Given this set of circumstances, one could expect employee reaction to be negative. Since the people on the project team affect most of the project information in one way or another, one could expect them to begin to distort that information, to shade things slightly in their favor whenever they get a chance.

This type of behavior could set up a self-defeating cycle. The project manager wants the information so that he knows what's going on and will not be surprised. On receiving the information, the project manager sends a negative message to team members. On receiving the negative message, team members begin to filter, shade, and "massage" the information that they give to the project manager. Because the manager is not receiving the right subsequent information, there is later a sudden surprise in the project. It seems that the very thing that the project manager sought to prevent was actually caused by the method of prevention. Therein lies the control system madness.

Consider now a different scenario. The project manager realizes that an activity is late. He makes assumption 4:

4. Some set of circumstances is causing the slippage. I wonder what these circumstances are?

With this assumption, the project manager works with the project team to review the decisions that have been made. Perhaps they underestimated, perhaps they are a bit slack, or perhaps both. If agreement on the causes of the delay is reached, the project manager now works with the team members to devise a solution. With this scenario, the manager has sent a very positive message to the team. This reinforces team spirit. Most likely, the team members will renew their vigor and use the team synergy to produce a solution. If harder work is called for, it is most likely that the team members will decide this for themselves.

The two scenarios given illustrate two different interactions with a control system. These two different scenarios were used to illustrate two major points about people and control. The first point is that the success of a system for controlling a project does not rely so much on the technical beauty of the system as it does on

1. the way the manager uses the information and
2. the way the manager relates to the project team. This includes making the investment in educating them in the why and how of control.

The second major point is that different sets of managerial assumptions about what causes people's behavior, and thus what control systems are for, produce different responses to the system on the part of the employees. That is, the assumptions of the project manager concerning the motivation of people often cause him to act in a certain way. This action affects the employees' reactions. The employees' reactions will affect the project manager. So it seems once again that the project manager gets back what he puts out.

It would thus appear that the key to effective project control systems revolves around managerial assumptions about people and how much they need to be controlled. These assumptions seem to arise from several different sources. The first is habit or organizational socialization. In essence, the project manager thinks a certain way because everyone else in the organization thinks that way. This type of conventional thinking is rarely helpful in the case of a "special" project. The second source is a lack of self-confidence on the part of the project manager. The third source is an assumption about what the motives of managers are and what the motives of employees are, and that somehow the motives of managers and employees are different.

To explore these assumptions in depth, we now cover the topics of perception and communication.

PERCEPTION

Limits to Our Perceptions

Our senses have a limited range. For example, we can only hear sounds with certain frequencies and above certain volumes. Some animals such as dogs can hear higher pitches. We do not perceive all of the factors (called "stimuli") in a situation in the same way. Experiments with color perception have led to the wide use of certain colors that are more easily perceived (such as "bright orange" hunting jackets and safety coats for workers on road construction crews). While there are various aids to improve our senses (e.g., glasses, microscopes, loudspeaker systems), many work situations create less than ideal conditions for perception.

Perceiving Other People

Many of our perceptions occur in situations in which the stimulus that we are observing is another person. Since much of management involves interacting with others, there are a variety of perceptual errors or misperceptions that can occur. For example, when we meet someone, we form a first impression. This initial perception tends to be lasting and to have an impact on the subsequent ways that we see and hear the other person. If our first impression of a subordinate is that he is very smart, we are likely to pay more attention to his ideas in future meetings. Research suggests that in many job interviews, the decision to hire or not to hire is made in the first four minutes of the interview. Even when we recognize (consciously) that first impressions are often not accurate, we are still influenced (unconsciously) in the ways that we perceive the individual.

In addition to the first impression, the most recent experience is important in our perception of another person. Internally, we develop an image or concept of a person, and we tend to perceive information that is consistent with the image and ignore information that contradicts it. For example, a manager who is seen as "hard and firm" may ask with concern about a fellow worker's absenteeism, but it may be perceived as applying pressure. We also use one perception as a *cue* to another factor that we can only infer. For example, many people initially felt that Jimmy Carter was honest and sincere, based only on the fact that he smiled a lot. Our impression or image of others tends to be fairly stable and resistant to change, and creates a bias in our perceptions.

Perceptual errors act to limit our ability to perceive other people accurately. Many stereotypes have been learned without any experience on our part. We may have beliefs about certain managers without ever having met them. Further, since we rarely think about our stereotypes, they interfere with our perceptions without our being aware of it. Our stereotypes also harm other people because they keep us from seeing them as they really are. Much of the process of perception allows us to simplify our environment so that we can better understand it. Yet, sometimes, we can simplify too much when we use a particular characteristic and try to generalize to others.

Another set of perceptual errors occurs when we perceive other people in relation to ourselves. For example, people tend to see others as more similar to themselves than they may really be. Some managers make the mistake of assuming that what motivates them will also motivate others.

Additional errors can occur when we have feelings about a person (based on an impression, a stereotype, or previous experience with that person). For example, if a person reminds us of someone else, we may expect the individual to behave in certain ways and misperceive his actual behavior. You may think that a new superior will be especially friendly and supportive because he has white hair like your uncle and a "kindly" smile, and you may perceive his behavior to be this way (more so than will other employees).

Frequently, we are aware that we feel threatened in a situation, but rarely do we recognize how our perceptions of the situation and other people are affected. Sometimes, we narrow the input of information to that relating directly to threat. There are a variety of ways in which we deceive ourselves when we feel defensive. In particular, when these processes are used, we are unaware (consciously) that we are doing so. We develop ways of not dealing with a situation rather than face it directly, and thus our preception is biased. For example, when we are angry, we may tend to find things wrong with the work of others (i.e., we displace the anger) which we would not have otherwise perceived or which might not even exist.

Selective Perception

When we perceive a situation, there are numerous stimuli that we can take in. In fact, there is too much information for us to deal with, so we develop a filtering process that allows us to ignore many of the stimuli and only perceive a smaller, more manageable number. We do not, however, randomly select information to perceive but do so on the basis of our personality and past experiences. This process of seeing things that we are familiar with and not seeing other things is called "selective perception." Every person, therefore, has a bias in his perceptions based on his own background and previous experiences in similar situations. Since no two people have had exactly the same experiences, the ways in which each of us selectively perceives will be different. Consider a discussion between a production supervisor (who has a degree in management, but no experience as a production worker) and a union steward. If they are talking about an employee who is frequently absent from work, the supervisor who is concerned about lost production may see the problem in terms of employee motivation and satisfaction (concepts that are taught in management courses). The union steward may talk about employee grievances and working conditions. This is not to suggest that either person is wrong, but rather that they perceive the situation differently, based on their selective processes.

The Effect of Perception on Decision Making
Processes and Behavior

To make decisions, we use information that we perceive in the particular situation. Yet, as we have discussed, our perceptions are not perfect. We systematically ignore, avoid, and misperceive based on our perceptual limits, our experiences and expectations, and a variety of other processes. We are especially biased about information that is threatening and makes us feel defensive, such as news that the project is late. When our perceptions are of other people (as is most often the case for a manager), we have additional problems of stereotypes and our image of the person. All of these affect decision making and behavioral reactions to control systems.

This summary of perceptual problems is not meant to be a pessimistic view of how poorly we perceive but is rather intended to reinforce the point that *different people will perceive a given situation in a variety of different ways.* There are implications for decisions making and action:

1. A decision and subsequent action are partially a function of perception—we can only decide based on what we have perceived.

2. One of the reasons that different people make different decisions and thus react differently to a situation is that they perceive the situation differently.
3. When more than one person is making a decision, the differences in perceptions need to be resolved before a good decision can be made (i.e., everyone has to have a common understanding of the problem).
4. Our expectations about the decision will influence the way we perceive the information. Another way to say this is that there are no decisions that are not affected by our perceptions.
5. There are no "objective decisions" since each of us selectively perceives based on his unique background and experiences.

   The implications for the project manager should be clear. Different people will react differently to any control system. A part of this reaction will be based on previous experiences with such systems. The project manager needs to be aware of this and then take steps to educate team members on the purpose of the project control system. The project manager must then behave in such a way that people believe that the control system is not in place to spy on them but rather is used as an early warning for needed changes.

COMMUNICATION

Another aspect of human interaction with control systems is upward filtering of information. The project manager's role as communicator is crucial and demanding. The usefulness of the control system for project management depends on the project manager obtaining information about problems, potential problems, and alternatives in time for effective redesign, rescheduling, or reallocation decisions. Because of the dynamic nature of most projects, standing formal reports contain only a fraction of what the project manager needs to know. Timely information is rarely delivered by way of accounting reports. This means that much of the needed information will usually come to the project manager from the people who have it—often in nonspecific formats, by nonspecific channels, and at nonspecific times.

According to Barndt (1981), the filtering of information in upward communication is highly probable in a project environment. He cites three reasons for this:

1. Project personnel do not always know what is important or unimportant. They may thus filter inadvertently.
2. The lack of formal channels or formats may also cause inadvertent filtering. In an unrehearsed conversation, it is easy to forget information or be led to another topic before concluding the last topic.
3. Project personnel may fear that they will be penalized for passing unpleasant news or information which they feel will reflect unfavorably upon themselves.

The extent to which these three areas of communication can be addressed will indicate the extent to which there will be full disclosure. The project manager must have a very clear idea of the specific information he needs to run the job. This will help him to very sharply focus his questions to the field. The tendencies toward inadvertent filtering can be partially negated by well-focused questions.

Studies have shown that upward filtering also decreases when there is a supportive organizational climate and there is a high level of trust between supervisors and subordinates. Four actions by the project manager aid in developing these conditions:

1. You get what you give. Subordinates respond in kind to the actions of the manager. It is, therefore, important that the manager who wants to receive information also practices giving information. Giving feedback usually helps to build a climate of trust. The finding by Burchette et al. (1977) is that trust in the superior is positively correlated with the percent of information received from the superior, the percent of time in contact with him, and the perceived accuracy of the information received from him.
2. The manager should visibly demonstrate a personal commitment to the project as a role model to the project team members. A personal commitment to the project, and hence a personal desire to see it succeed, can provide an incentive for more complete upward disclosure.

3. The project manager must take time to listen. Communication becomes sloppy and incomplete when the subordinate begins to feel that the manager is not listening. People begin to take a "what's the use" attitude, and upward communication grinds to a halt.
4. The project manager needs to consistently reward open and upward communication through acknowledgment, praise, and public credit.

These are fairly specific steps, but the general background notions should not be forgotten. The first is telling why as well as what. The second is having team members pass information for the good of the team and for the attainment of their personal value, not just for the good of the project or project manager.

Attempting to tell people everything that you need has some negative consequences. The first is that you probably do not know exactly what you need and thus cannot specify correctly. When the needed information is not forthcoming, there may be a tendency to blame the subordinate. Doing this could set up a negative regenerative cycle that would further hamper communication.

Since you may not know what you need, there may be a tendency to overcompensate and ask for everything. This will cause needless volumes of reports to be generated and not read. In addition, the information will come despite changes in circumstances that make such reports unnecessary.

By far, however, the largest negative consequence is that people are generating reports, or otherwise passing on information, and they do not know why. The whole exercise takes on the air of a ritual. People go through the motions; they feel that there is a reason for it all, but they do not know what the reason is.

The message here seems clear. The project manager, in an effort to increase upward communication, needs to increase downward communication, particularly in supplying reasons for the requested information. In designing the information flow for the project, the manager should be able to sit with team members and indicate both what information is needed and why it is needed—usually for redesign, rescheduling, or reallocation. All of these processes help the team and thus help each team member realize the value he will receive from successful project completion. Therefore, the passing of relevant information becomes instrumental in the achievement of personal value. When this is the case, people will constantly search for information to pass on to the project manager and will filter out those things that they know are not necessary. However, they cannot filter unless they know why the information is necessary.

So there is a double incentive for telling people why information is needed. The first is that it is the only way for team members to relate the information request to the attainment of personal value. If this is not done, it will be seen as a chore. The second benefit is that it helps people filter unnecessary information so that there is not a flood of data coming at the project manager.

MANAGEMENT CONTROL

Up to this point we have been discussing project control and people, those aspects of control interaction that are internal to the project. Now we move to a second major area of control which comes under the heading of management control. This control is mainly external to the project. It can take many forms and have many consequences. Once again we are not concerned directly with the actual control system but rather how people use and interact with the control system, what some of the negative consequences of these interactions might be, and how the project manager can decrease the effects of the negative consequences.

The area of management control will be examined under two broad headings. The first is direct top management intervention. The second, more subtle heading is indirect organizational control.

Top Management Intervention

No project exists in a vacuum. Projects exist within organizations, the top management of which is also attempting to attain some personal value. Project charters are usually given by top management. In addition, many projects exist as part of a plan for strategy implementation formulated by top management. For these reasons, top management definitely has a need to know how the project is progressing. Thus, it becomes part of the control system.

Most organizations have standard operating procedures for reporting to top management. Most information to top management takes the form of regular written or verbal reports. For many in top management, however, project control is interpreted as project direction. They may think that it is their job to tell team members what to do—to get involved in the actual execution of the project. Part of the job of the project manager then becomes to protect the team from this type of interference. Successful project completion depends on the ability of the team members to execute their tasks as they see fit. This concept should be made clear to top management at the beginning of the project and reinforced by subsequent behavior on the part of the project manager.

The benefits of group synergy will not be realized if anyone is constantly interfering with the workings of the group. Thus the entire team should decide early on how to handle direct requests or orders on the part of top management. The usual format is that knowledge of such requests is immediately relayed to the project manager, who must then take a firm stand, often counter to the wishes of top management. This is often not easy, but it seems necessary.

The larger concept here is that top management and the project team form two components of a system. The system will only function correctly if the relationship between them is balanced. That is, the project team must accept the authority that top management exerts. To balance this, top management must accept the authority that the team exerts. Thus, while top management has the authority to state the final goal and to penalize people if those goals are not met, the project team has the authority to determine how those goals are going to be met. Without this sort of mutual balance of power, the system will eventually break down.

In accepting this authority, each side must also accept the responsibility of informing the other of the consequences of the other's actions. Because each part of this system is attending to different aspects of the entire organization, it may not be aware of the full consequences of its actions. One side may inadvertently cause difficult problems for the other without being aware of this.

For example, suppose top management asks the team to release a member without replacement. Good managers should always be ready to explain why they are making such a request. In response, the team should be able to calculate the impact of this loss in terms of schedule, quality of final product, and other areas, and then ask top management which functions should be dropped or which deadlines should be altered as a result of its decision. When this is done, top management will be informed of the consequences of its decisions, and the team will be able to reschedule with the lower asset level.

Indirect Organizational Control

Complaints about indirect organizational control are often voiced as complaints against "staff." This is a subtle type of control which is not really control in the sense of information for corrective action but rather control in the form of expectations of behavior. These expectations are both for the behavior of the people on the project and for the behavior of the people on the staff.

The normal manifestation is that well-meaning people exert whatever power they have to persuade others to act in the manner to which they have become accustomed. In Chapter 5, we discussed how culture is essentially a set of expectations. People deal with each other based on these expectations. If the expectations are not met, the tendency is to use whatever power is available in order to force the person to behave as expected.

Another manifestation occurs when there is adoption of a new management style that most everyone supports. However, staff people must still fill out their old forms and produce their old reports or perform their old functions. They normally do this in the old way. As this is carried out, it often sends mixed messages to the people on the project.

One project manager related an example to me concerning the format of a kickoff dinner. The yearly sales kickoff meeting was normally a corporate affair. There was a corporate staff department that took care of most of the arrangements. However, after the adoption of a project management system, top management felt that individual project kickoffs would be more appropriate. They informed the project manager that he was to plan his own affair. However, a few weeks later, a package arrived from the staff department instructing the manager on what to do for the dinner, who to have speak, and who to invite. It seems that the staff department proceeded as before and merely left the arranging (i.e., place and time) to the project manager. This was not in the spirit of the top management directive. However, it was interpreted that way by the staff department because nobody had told them otherwise. This combination of events sent a mixed message to the project manager and caused much consternation.

This is just one example of the type of unnecessary friction that can arise when the project manager works one way and the majority of the people in the organization work another. There are many smaller interactions with other people every day in which the "others" have been told to expect a certain type of behavior and then treat everyone "as if" they are the same. If the team is attempting to behave differently, friction can arise. Day after day of this friction has a tendency to wear people down as frustration increases. A normal result in that the old ways prevail and the project members are no longer able to enjoy their special management process.

CONTROL SYSTEMS AS IF PEOPLE MATTERED

Cammann and Nadler (1976) have studied the effects of control systems on people. They differentiate between external and internal control.

External Control

The external control strategy is based on the assumption that subordinates are motivated primarily by external rewards and need to be controlled by their supervisors. This type of control system has three aspects. First, the standards must be made relatively difficult in order to stretch the subordinates. Second, the measures have to be relatively people-proof to prevent individuals from manipulating the system. Third, rewards need to be directly and openly tied to performance. A quota sales system is an example of an external control system.

An external strategy can have various effects. On the one hand, a great deal of energy will be spent on the measured areas. The quota will most likely be attained. On the other hand, there may be some undesirable results. First, this type of system may not create commitment to doing a better job. There is always a temptation to manipulate the measures rather then commit to doing the job more effectively. Second, the strategy may result in misdirected efforts as people put their energies into what is measured and neglect behavior that is not measured. Not all vital behavior is measurable. Third, the external strategy may tend to reduce the flow of information, especially the negative information that is so vital for rescheduling. Finally, this strategy may bring about excessive caution as people shun risks so they will look good in the measured areas.

Internal Motivation

This is the strategy of goal control where management assumes that subordinates can be motivated by the feelings of accomplishment, achievement, recognition, and self-esteem that come from having performed well. This type of control system requires that goals be set participatively. This means that the people who are responsible for achieving the goals are given some influence over the nature of these goals. Second, it requires that measures be used for joint problem solving rather than for punishment or blame. Finally, although rewards are tied to performance, they are not tied to one or two specific measures. Rather, there is a stress on entire job performance, including the ability to work well with the team.

This type of system has the potential for generating high commitment to goal achievement along with high motivation and performance. There is overall high commitment to the team and little game playing with measures. There is generally a large flow of valid information because this is seen as essential to goal achievement.

At the same time, such a strategy may have what can be seen as undesirable effects. For one, the comparatively loose nature of the system means that management will have less control over the behavior of subordinates. In addition, the information provided is for problem solving and not for evaluation. It is difficult to use such information as the basis for giving rewards. Finally, some individuals may not respond to the participative process because of differences in working style of personality.

Most of the objections to the participative style seem somewhat trivial. For example, there are also individuals who will not respond to external control systems. The real question seems to come down to the project manager's self-concept and self-confidence. All of the rational arguments for internal control systems are useless to the manager who does not have the self-confidence to allow workers to determine their own work behavior. Without this self-confidence, the manager will feel uneasy with internal control because he will not really believe that it works. He may believe that there is a hidden flaw and that this will be discovered by his superiors, or he may feel that he will be seen as weak by his peers. Whatever the cause, the manager contemplating goal control should first check his self-confidence before proceeding.

Goal Control: The Complete Project Manager's Control System

A goal control system is built by stressing results, teamwork, and personal growth for personal value attainment for all people on the team. This means stressing output rather than input, allowing team members to formulate and solve their own problems their own way, and allowing people to make mistakes so they can experience personal growth and learning. Some of the details of the system follow:

1. The first step is to stress results, the results the subordinates achieve through methods they develop, either by themselves or by working with their peers.
2. The next step is for the project manager to refuse to do the subordinates' work for them. By doing this, the project manager will enable the team members to grow in terms of their ability to make decisions under conditions of uncertainty. The project manager's contact with subordinates should be centered around negotiation of performance standards and review of progress reports on the results they are achieving. When performances fall short of standards, the task of the project manager is to remind people that they have a problem and that he is interested in how they are going to solve it.
3. Refer people with problems to peers. The most effective pressure to achieve goals is peer pressure. This is especially true on a project because of the known interdependencies. If one team member fails, then sooner or later all fail. It is thus in the interest of each team member to help each other so that the entire project will be a success. Thus when a person comes to the project office saying there is a problem, the correct response is to agree and to indicate that you are interested in seeing how he and other team members work it out. Do not permit dependency on the project manager to become the standard problem solving technique.
4. Deal with each problem as a learning situation. Unfortunately, it seems that calling something a "learning situation" seems to im-

bue it with a negative connotation. Yet such situations are exactly what is necessary if the goal control system is to work. If people have a problem, they need to understand why they have a problem, as well as be able to formulate a solution. All too often, the project manager uses a problem situation to show his problem solving expertise. If this is the approach, team members cannot be expected to learn and grow. It is true that the project manager is ultimately responsible for choosing the right answer to a problem, but he should not be responsible for formulating the solutions.

5. Concentrate review meetings on progress, completed problems solved, and who helped whom. Too often, review meetings turn into problem solving activities. This takes the emphasis off results and puts it on problem areas. It also allows dependency on the project manager for problem solving. By concentrating the meetings on progress, only those problems solved, and who helped in solving those problems, the project manager reinforces the emphasis on results, personal growth, and teamwork.

6. The project manager's major task is to implement the rescheduling or other redesigning elements thought necessary by the project team. This must be done through interaction with top management. The project manager should concentrate on this and on the task of reducing the opposing forces of the "staff." This is how the project manager can be of most benefit to the team. If this can be done correctly, the project will most likely control itself.

REFERENCES

Barndt, S. "Upward Communication Filtering in the Project Management Environment," *Project Management Quarterly,* March 1981.

Burchette, H. T., Porter, R. O., Blalack, R. O., and Davis, H. J. "Gatekeeping and Upward Communication: Another Test of Three Contributing Factors," *Annual Meeting of the Academy of Management,* 1977.

Cammann, C. and Nadler, D. "Fit Control Systems to Your Managerial Style," *Harvard Business Review,* January–February 1976.

Lewin, K. *A Dynamic Theory of Personality.* New York: McGraw-Hill, 1935.

"GIVE THE KID A NUMBER": AN ESSAY ON THE FOLLY AND CONSEQUENCES OF TRUSTING YOUR DATA*

Robert J. Graham

> The Government are very keen on amassing statistics—they collect them, add them, raise them to the nth power, take the cube root and prepare wonderful diagrams. But what you must never forget is that every one of these figures comes in the first instance from the . . . (village watchman), who just puts down what he pleases. [Stamp, 1929—quoted in Bogdan and Ksander, 1980]

Most Management Scientists consider themselves realists. We believe there is a real world "out there," that natural laws do indeed exist, that we can discover these laws, and that we can build mathematical models to study these laws. We draw heavily on the physical, biological, and mathematical sciences to help construct our world views. One of the most significant symbols in our world is data—the stuff forming the very foundation of our models, whose very existence confirm the reality that we assume. Data are numbers that reflect the hard facts of life—or so I was led to believe during my process of initiation to this field. However, in the years since my release from graduate school, I have yet to encounter any situation when the data reflected any agreed-upon "reality." The usual situation is that there are many versions of reality and the data provided reflect an approximation of one version of this reality—maybe. Most likely, the data reflect what most people wish was reality or what people want you to believe is reality. The purpose of this essay is to review some of the common assumptions and misperceptions made about data and to examine the folly and consequences of believing the concept that objective data indeed exist.

SOME ASSUMPTIONS ABOUT DATA

Assumption 1. Data reflects a constant reality.

This assumption relies on the notion that data are the result of some mechanical or standard biological process that is unchanging from year to year. This comes from the physical science "natural laws" view of the world. For example, if we are counting the number of people born in a year we can assume that all human beings (except one) came about via the same process.

This assumption is clearly not true for any measures that we take on a business organization. All organizations are composed of people interacting in a social process and the data are a result of this social process, not a

---

*Copyright © 1982, *Interfaces* 12(2) pp. 40–44. The Institute of Management Sciences, 290 Westminster Street, Providence, Rhode Island 02903.

mechanical process. This social process may be fairly standard from year to year but it always involves slightly different people with slightly different feelings, motives, and perspectives. These changes in people can yield changes in data which are often misinterpreted to signify a change in business circumstances but which really only reflect a change in the social fabric of the organization.

As an example, let us examine an area that most people consider fairly mundane and mechanical; namely, inventory. Many people, particularly financial types, think that inventory reflects the result of doing business and nothing more. However, as I have elsewhere argued [Graham, 1978], there are people who have strong feelings about inventory and who, for reasons of their own, want inventory levels to be one way or another. I am thinking here of the difference between the marketing types that want inventory "high" and the finance types who want inventory "low." If a company changes presidents from a finance type to a marketing type, it is almost inevitable that inventory levels will rise. This rise will reflect only the change in the social fabric of the organization and, in particular, the new president's feeling that more inventory is better than less inventory. In essence, the new president has redefined the reality of the business situation and has made adjustments to fit his definition of reality. Thus, last year's and this year's inventory levels are a result of two different social processes conducted under two different definitions of reality. In this situation there is no valid comparison that can be made other than to say one level is different from the other.

To make matters worse, I need to point out that people are not the only things in organizations that change from year to year. There are also changes in accounting systems, reward systems, incentive and bonus plans, as well as organization structure changes. All of these factors influence the social process of the organization and thus the data that are reported about it. I have argued elsewhere that data on any organization are valid only as far back as the last change in accounting procedures [Graham, 1976]. Others have argued that data categories change with company reorganization so that data are only valid as far back as the last reorganization. Bogdan and Ksander [1980] argue that all data are a result of a social process, so that any change in the social organization of the firm will change the way data are recorded. Thus, data on an organization are only valid as far back as the last major change in personnel, the last reorganization, or the last change in accounting procedures, whichever was most recent. In any organization worth studying, at least one of the above changes will occur in any given year. Thus, data does not reflect a constant reality but rather a quite dynamically changing reality. My argument is that using such data for your models, without a thorough understanding of changing realities, is pure folly. Data must be viewed through a glass darkly.

Assumption 2. People are behaving according to the rules.

Many organizations have elaborate management control systems, complete with forms, norms, standards, and the like, which spin out data that claim to represent what people are doing in an organization. To this assertion our British colleagues would answer a resounding "Rubbish." Their answer would be so sincere because England is a prime example of what happens when a governing body attempts to measure (and tax or report) everything that a group of people are doing. The unusual result of any control system seems to be that people quickly learn how to "fiddle" the system for their own purposes. England has been called a nation of fiddlers as various schemes have been devised to keep income and possessions out of view of the taxman. As an example, there seem to be very few British executives that own their own automobiles. What happens is that the companies own the automobiles and "lend" them to the executives for a fee. Thus, any reporting on the percentage of Britishers who own automobiles would be, as they say, rubbish.

I have witnessed the same type of behavior occurring in numerous business organizations. The typical example is for people in the home office to produce reams of data proported to reflect decisions made in the field according to a specific set of rules and procedures. One or two days in the field usually reveals that the reporting system is a total illusion and that people in the field are doing what they damn well please and then filling out the forms to reflect what they think the home office wants to see.

Probably the most thoroughly documented case of this type of behavior is in Wolcott's book *Teacher vs Technocrat* [1977]. In this report, a raft of data indicated the success of a new teaching method. The technocrats (home-office types) reported that the teachers loved the new method. But Wolcott spent some time with the teachers (in the field) and found that they hated the method and did not really use it. However, they dutifully filled in the forms to reflect what the technocrats wanted to hear. So the lesson from this assumption is to never believe what a manager tells you his people do, especially if he claims behavior is done according to the rule book. The only way to find out what really happens is to go "in the field" and spend some time with the people actually doing the work. It often helps to drink a few beers with them also—a couple of brews tend to help people remember the truth. Without this type of first-hand data, your models will be built on fiction and the results will reflect it.

Assumption 3. People will do what they say for the reasons they say.

We are all in the business of prediction, and one of the biggest problems that we run into is building predictive models based on the assumption that people are going to do what they told us they were going to do and for the reasons they told us they were going to do it. Experience seems to indicate that many people have little idea of how they will behave in the future, let alone know the factors that would cause such behavior. Models based on the uncritical use of such data seem destined for failure. For example, the field of marketing is filled with models that attempt to predict behavior based on people's stated intentions [see Graham, 1981]. The failure of these models indicates the depth of the problem of predicting behavior in all but the most mundane situations.

Determining the reasons for behavior is equally difficult. Much organizational behavior is done for political reasons and thus defies rational analysis. However, rarely is behavior justified on political grounds. As Boissevain [1974, p. 6] has remarked:

> Naked motives of crude self-interest can never be brought forward to justify action to others. Pragmatic action is dressed up in normative clothes to make it acceptable.

This is similar to Maruyama's [1978] notion of the cassette response. As individuals learn the organizational culture they learn which responses are appropriate for various circumstances. These responses are stored away, as on tape cassettes, and as the questions are asked, individuals merely select a "cassette" that seems appropriate, plug it into their brain, and an answer comes forward. Assuming that this answer has anything to do with the real reasons for behavior is probably a mistake. So once again my argument seems to be that unless you take the time to really know the people you are dealing with, or whose behavior you are trying to model, the data for your model will be based on fiction.

Assumption 4. Production of data is not affected by organizational politics.

This assumption is totally false; people are *not* passive participants in an organization. They have goals and purposes. People manufacture, massage, filter, and shade data for various reasons. This is particularly true in an organization that is "run by the numbers." If you are using data produced by someone else you had better be certain that you understand how and why they were produced. Otherwise you may be in for a shock.

A recent story by Kaufman [1981] in the *New York Times* illustrates the point nicely. It seems that in times of tight money and a slow housing market, most people benefit by keeping up the illusion that housing prices are rising. Something called a buy-down scheme has been created to facilitate the illusion. To quote Kaufman:

> Buy downs do not actually affect the asking prices, but they do lower the price received by the seller in order to make the home more affordable to buyers.

That is, a house that is reported to have sold for $100,000 may only net the builder $90,000 due to his $10,000 buy-down payment to the bank. The $100,000 figure is a phoney but it is the official figure. Uncritical use of such data would produce results just as phoney as the official figure.

The above is not an isolated incident; this type of data "shading" happens daily. Inventories are valued on the day most advantageous for tax purposes, not the day that is most representative of true value. I have seen quite a bit of data manufactured by people simply to keep some government bureaucrat off their back. Bailey [1977, p. 29] reports a story in which a group of university professors instructed the administrators to "fix the figures" to show the State that they were indeed using all of the space under their control. Often when a model builder approaches the accounting department, it might take the attitude of "give the kid a number" [see Woolsey, 1975] just to get that person out of the office. The list could go on and on.

The main theme here is that people have motives and purposes and so when they have the ability to influence data they will most likely influence it to suit their purposes. Since all data are produced by people, we can assume that all data are biased. It behooves the model builder to understand just what that bias is and how it affects the data.

WHAT TO DO

Writers of iconoclastic pieces like this usually end by pontificating on what future generations should do in order to be better off in some way. Such a list of suggestions is usually agreed upon by the old timers, since it has happened to them, and largely ignored by the youngsters, since they feel it won't happen to them. Besides, most people can see through the rationalized argument to the true sentiment that is being expressed—namely that you (the reader) should be more like me (the writer). Thus it seems that such lists are largely for purposes of self-aggrandizement. I am not above any of this so my list is presented below. I only mention my feelings on the purposes of such lists in order to supply some of the salt that should be taken with its ingestion.

Learn accounting. Accountants produce data for a variety of reasons, not all of which are devious. If you are counting on the accounting department for your data, you should be well aware of the gyrations they go through to produce it.

Learn the business. Some people think that OR/MS techniques are generic, that something like inventory models can be applied to all inventory situations. But it is easy to see that your standard EOQ model does not work well with perishable goods. It helps to know the business before you build the model.

Learn about people. Be cognizant of what makes people tick and how they define reality. Do not just ask for a number but ask what it means to the people who produced it. Always be aware that your reality is not their reality.

Learn the political and financial games. Find out who is trying to do what to whom to give an indication of how one department may shade its data in one direction or another. Another indicator of shading is whether the company as a whole wants to look good or bad on paper.

Check it out. Finally, I think that for the good of the profession it would be helpful if we all adopted the methods of many journalists concerning statements made by people. It goes something like this:

Even if your mother says she loves you, CHECK IT OUT!

REFERENCES

Bailey, F. G., 1977, *Morality and Expediency: The Folklore of Academic Politics,* Basil Blackwell, Oxford.

Bogdan, R. and Ksander, M., 1980, "Policy Data as a Social Process: A Qualitative Approach to Quantitative Data," *Human Organization* Vol. 39, No. 4.

Boissevain, J., 1974, *Friends of Friends,* Basil Blackwell, Oxford.

Graham, R. J., 1976, "Use of Computer Models for Problem Realization," *Interfaces* Vol. 6, No. 4.

Graham, R. J., 1978, "EOQ—Once More with Feeling," *Interfaces* Vol. 9, No. 1.

Graham, R. J., 1981, "The Role of Perception of Time in Consumer Research," *Journal of Consumer Research* Vol. 7, March.

Kaufman, M. W., 1981, "The Coming Collapse is Already Here," *The New York Times* August 9, 1981, Section 3, p. 2.

Maruyama, M., 1978, "Endogenous Research and Polyocular Anthropology," in R. E. Holloman and S. Arutionov (eds.), *Perspectives on Ethnicity,* Mouton, The Hague.

Wolcott, H., 1977, *Teacher vs Technocrat,* University of Washington Press.

Woolsey, R. E. D., 1975, "The Measure of MS/OR Application or Let's Hear It for the Bean Counters," *Interfaces* Vol. 5, No. 2.

8
Matrix Organization

We trained hard . . . . But it seemed that every time
we were beginning to form up into teams
we would be reorganized.
I was to learn later in life that we tend to meet any
new situation by reorganizing: and what a wonderful
method it can be for creating the illusion of progress
while producing confusion, inefficiency and
demoralization.

Petronius Arbiter
Greek Navy, 210 B.C.

As project management grew in practice, many people felt that a new form of organization was necessary so that projects could be better run and receive higher status in organizations. This chapter is a brief review of the development of project-oriented or matrix organizations.

The chapter begins by outlining some of the effects of organizational design on the behavior of people in the organization. From this viewpoint, various organizational forms are reviewed along with their advantages and disadvantages. The progression is followed from the standard functional organization to the matrix form of organization.

The matrix or project form is not for everyone. Experience proves it to be difficult for people. Some human problems with the new forms are thus reviewed. In addition, excerpts from a manager talking about his experience in such an organization are included in the end-of-chapter reading (Stuntz, 1983).

THE ROLE OF ORGANIZATIONAL STRUCTURE

Up to this point, we have mainly been examining the relationships of people on the project team to each other and the relationship between team members and the project manager. In Chapter 7, we began to examine relationships outside of the team by looking at the effect of management control and the perspective of people in management. In this chapter, we examine the effect of organization structure on the project team as well as the effect of the structure on the interaction of the project team with the rest of the organization.

The term "organization structure" is often associated with the form of the organization shown on the organizational chart. While this may be the symbol of organizational structure, it is not the main concern in this chapter. We will consider organizational structure to include authority delegation, the criteria by which people are grouped together, the rules and procedures that determine what the people in various groups attend to, and the patterns of interaction that are fostered by all of these. That is, since organizations are structured to induce various sorts of behavior, we are interested in the factors that tend to encourage or prevent the behavior desired.

Throughout the previous discussions we have assumed a functional organization in which people are grouped according to their functions such as accounting, marketing, etc. Special projects tend to try to cut across these functions and to group people by project. If only a few small projects were being performed in an organization, there would probably be no need to initiate any changes in the structure. As the importance of projects begins to grow, however, top management may find that it wishes to have the organizational groupings reflect the importance of the projects.

One option is to move away from standing departments to a pure project form. With a pure project form, all people would be grouped by projects and there would be few functional departments. This is the form used by many consulting firms that work on a project-by-project basis. The budgets are controlled by the project managers, and people who cannot find work on the various projects are not retained by the firm.

There are, however, advantages to having standing departments in order to maintain continuity and to achieve whatever economies of scale may exist in the organization. Thus it may be advantageous to have both project and functional groupings. The matrix organization is an attempt to structure just such a mixture of groupings.

Structure is not organization. Any organization is composed of people interacting to produce particular outputs. The organizational structure, however, is a part of our cognitive equipment. It tells us who is in an organization and gives an indication of what each does. It is a part of our perceptual screen, so it acts as a map of organizational functioning and interactions. As such, it is key to the forming of our mutual expectancies, as discussed in Chapter 5. Organizational structure helps to indicate the standards by which we should interact with others. It helps to indicate the proper behavior for various groups. Thus is it part of the culture. Since structure affects our interaction with people, structure is a part of the organization.

Changing the organizational structure does not change the organization per se. After the structural change, there are normally still most of the same people producing the same products with the same technology. Real organizational change takes place when people begin to interact with each other differently or when they begin to think differently about their role and function in the organization. Since most changes in structure affect people's interactions with, and orientations towards, others, we say that structural change affects organizational culture.

Originally, organizations were structured to accrue the benefits of specialization and the so-called economies of scale. The assembly line of Henry Ford took this concept to its logical conclusion. In this situation, the product and the manufacturing processes were well known. Each person had a specific task which contributed in some way to the whole. Each person did his part and only his part. This is an example of task specialization with authority centralization.

Specialization gives people a certain myopic perspective. That is, they only see a small part of the entire job. They are told to be concerned only with their part in the entire process, and they normally respond accordingly. For example, people in the advertising department may only be concerned with positioning a product in the consumer's mind. They may have little concern with how the product was conceived, engineered, or manufactured. Their perspective is to attend to one part of the product only. This may indeed by myopic, but it is the price that must be paid for the benefits accrued. As long as the benefits of specialization outweigh the price of narrow perspective, that type of organizational structure seems a natural one to use.

The problems of specialization and centralization are most evident during periods of rapid change. When change occurs rapidly, people in organizations must make decisions quickly. The people in the lower part of the organization are normally the closest to the changes, and they are often in the best position to make rapid decisions. However, with centralization, normal decision making must go up a chain of command which takes the decision far away from contact with the problem. By the time the decision returns, the day may be lost.

So the solution seems to be to attempt to push decision making down the line to the lowest possible level. This becomes authority decentralization. The problem with this is that people down below in the organization may have a narrow perspective, by design. That is, before decentralization, they were told to tend only their own section of the total operation. This can often result in what are called short-sighted decisions. The need then is to attempt to widen the perspective of the people at the bottom and at the middle of the organization. This is done with a combination of task enrichment and authority decentralization.

The Role of Decentralization

A firm is said to be centralized to the extent that authority is concentrated at relatively high levels of management. In contrast, the amount of authority which is delegated or dispersed to lower levels is said to represent the extent to which the firm is decentralized. Most firms begin with centralized authority in the hands of the founders. As the firms grow and expand, decentralization comes about by sheer necessity. The people at the top can no longer make all of the decisions that are necessary. The degree of decentralization in a firm is thus said to be greater:

The greater the number of decisions made lower in the hierarchy
The more important the decisions made lower in the hierarchy
The more functions affected by decisions made at lower levels
The less checking required on decisions

Graham (1982) has found the advantages of authority decentralization in the areas of efficiency, flexibility, initiative, and management development. It is very challenging and motivating for managers to make decisions regarding problems and solutions in their own department. Good decisions require a broad perspective, and managers develop this perspective in decentralized organizations as they gain competence and confidence.

The disadvantages of decentralization are seen to lie in the areas of control, duplication of certain functions like inventory, and less use of centralized expertise (i.e., "staff"). Control is probably seen as the main drawback. Many top managers are not fluent in all aspects of the organization. When people are unsure of themselves, they tend to want to overcontrol the situations for which they are responsible. Retaining most decision making authority allows them to keep this control. In addition, control is seen as an element of power and top managers are often interested in maintaining as much power as possible.

Thus the dilemma of decentralization is that most of the advantages accrue to lower level managers while most of the disadvantages accrue to upper level managers. Since it is the upper level managers who make the decentralization decisions, they often decide in their own favor. This is fine for the short run, but for the longer run, the lack of managers with sufficient perspective will hurt the organization. It may be wise for the organization to consider a form that encourages decentralization.

The matrix form of organization represents just such an attempt at widening perspective by using organizational design. The matrix design consists essentially of two organizational forms overlaid on each other. The first is the traditional functional organization in which each person is identified as being a member of a particular and specific department. The second dimension is a set of projects. Each person is also identified as being a member of one or more project teams. Being a member of a project team normally enriches the tasks of people in functional departments. The exposure to people from other departments helps to widen their perspective and acts to lessen interdepartmental hostility. If this can be done along with authority decentralization, a vibrant and creative organization will most likely result.

FORMS OF ORGANIZATION: FUNCTIONAL TO MATRIX

Functional Departmentalization

The phrase "Functional to Matrix" is not meant to imply that moving to a matrix is somehow dysfunctional. What is implied is that there has been a movement away from functional forms as organizations increased in complexity. A review of the change of forms is given here.

Organizational forms usually begin with functional departmentalization, since this is the most appropriate form for small to medium-sized firms. A functionally structured firm groups its activities into separate units or departments, each of which undertakes a distinctive function. This form is shown structurally in Figure 8-1. Specialization and focused concentration on functional activities are apparent.

The principal strength of the functional design is its utilization of specialized inputs. The positive result is a gain in the administrative economies of scale. For example, once all engineers are organized around a central engineering department, it is possible to differentiate among electrical, mechanical, industrial, and other specializations within the larger engineering category. This type of organization is particularly effective when a firm is a mass producer of items for sale from stock, such as washers, ovens, and television sets. Further advantages of this organizational form include the following:

- It offers a simple communication and decision network.
- It facilitates measurement of functional output and results.
- It simplifies training of functional specialists.
- It gives status to major functional areas.
- It preserves strategic control at the top management level.

The major shortcoming of the functional design is the myopic perspective fostered by concentrating on functional activities. Under these circumstances, interdepartmental cooperation emerges as a problem and departmental interests begin to take precedence over broader organizational goals. This process has been documented by Price (1968) who, in a study of the impact of different forms of departmentalization on organizational performance, found that the functional form not only hampered cooperation because it provided

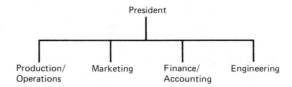

Figure 8-1. Firm divided into departments by function.

no interoccupational contact, but also fostered a parochial emphasis on functional objectives with a minimum appreciation of, or concern for, overall organizational goals.

Other disadvantages include:

- Cost of coordination between departments can be high.
- Employee identification with departments makes change difficult.
- Preparation of broadly trained managers is limited.
- Interdepartmental rivalry and conflict are encouraged.
- Client satisfaction can be lower than that obtained with other methods of organization.

As the firm grows and the product lines are diversified, the weaknesses of the functional form usually become apparent. If growth and change are desired, firms often switch to a product form of organization.

Product Departmentalization

Grouping activities on the basis of related product markets was pioneered by the Du Pont company at the turn of the century. A similar form under the name of federal decentralization was pioneered by General Motors in the 1920s. As both of these organizations grew in size, they encountered two major structural problems: their operational responsiveness was inadequate for the demands of their markets, and they lacked the breadth of perspective necessary to efficiently coordinate increasingly specialized inputs (Bedeian, 1984, p. 71).

The response was an organization structure whose primary basis for grouping was by product rather than by function. With product departmentalization, each major product line is administered through a separate and semiautonomous division. To this end, product specialists are grouped to perform all duties necessary to produce an individual product or service. A majority of the world's largest corporations are structured at their upper levels according to one of the numerous variations on the product departmentalization pattern.

One of the major benefits of the product organization is that it "is better adapted to accommodate growth through diversification than is the earlier functional design because it permits the coordination across functions to take place at lower levels of the hierarchy, and thus decisions can be made closer to the source of the relevant information" (Davis, 1979, p. 196). In this way, divisions can be made responsible for operating decisions while headquarters remains responsible for strategic decisions.

Additional benefits of the product form include:

- Product departments can be measured as profit centers.
- It facilitates coordination between functions for rapid response.
- It contributes flexibility to the structure since product departments can be added or dropped with relative ease.
- It focuses on client needs and thus leads to greater customer service.
- It helps to develop broadly trained managers.

The major disadvantages of the product form seem to stem from the problems associated with coordination across product areas. Lack of clarity in responsibilities and decrease in professional contacts between product specialists are likely to occur as structural complexity increases. Since numerous contacts with others are known to be essential in maintaining creativity, the flow of creative ideas may also decrease. As the product form contributes to a lack of clarity in the responsibilities of specific functional areas, a duplication of services may occur.

Matrix Organization

The product form of organization makes the first step towards being more responsive to changes in the organizational environment. That step is the inherent decentralization contained in the product groups. Where products are relatively stable and product changes are few, that form allows for high response to customers and corresponding customer satisfaction. In the end, however, one has a functional structure for each product group, with its inherent problems with change. The matrix form of organization is an attempt to attack the problem of organizational existence in an environment of rapid change.

The matrix organizational form attempts to cross the product and the functional approaches to departmentalization in order to get the best (and avoid the worst) of each. It does so by simultaneously maximizing an organization's needs for specialization and coordination.

The distinguishing feature of the matrix form is that functional and product lines of authority are overlaid to form a grid or matrix, as shown in Figure 8-2. As a consequence, many employees belong simultaneously to two groups. The first is a functional or specialist group, and the second is a product or project group. In addition, the employees may report to two or more superiors—a permanent manager in the functional group and one or more project managers in the project group.

Project managers and functional managers thus have separate but complementary responsibilities. Functional managers are responsible for developing and deploying, in the form of skilled personnel, a

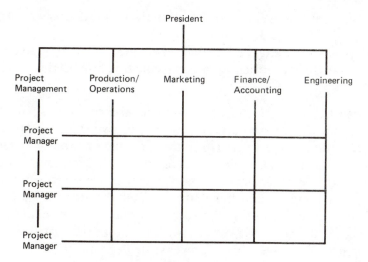

Figure 8-2. Matrix organization.

technical resource. Project managers are responsible for project completion. A typical matrix organizational chart is shown in Figure 8-2.

Matrix departmentalization is an especially flexible and responsive approach to organizational design. It is particularly adaptable to fluctuating work loads, while it allows the firm to respond to various sectors of the environment that are critical to its success. As projects are completed, the project teams are disbanded and the team members return to their respective functional areas for reassignment.

It is also significant that research suggests that the interdisciplinary nature of project teams contributes to a high rate of new product innovations (Kolodny, 1980). To the extent that the project teams are able to maintain autonomy while still maintaining access to the functional resources of a larger organization, they incorporate the behavioral and structural advantages of a small company with a big company support system.

Other advantages of the matrix organization are:

- It establishes the project manager as the focal point for all matters pertaining to an individual project.
- It makes possible the maximum use of a limited pool of functional specialists.
- It makes specialized functional assistance equally available to all projects.
- It provides a home base for functional specialists as ongoing projects are completed.
- It provides experience for lower managers in running a complex firm in which conflicting interests must be balanced.

Naturally, there are drawbacks to the matrix form. The most serious seems to be based on the existence of two separate operating systems within a single firm. This introduces the possibility of serious command conflict, particularly where authority intersects. While in theory a balance of power is called for between the project and the functional managers, it often happens that the project manager's power amounts to little more than persuasiveness (Dunne et al., 1978). Davis and Lawrence (1978) have also found that the matrix form of dual command is vulnerable to power struggles, indecision, and what they termed "groupitis." An organization contemplating such a form should be ready to deal with the inherent conflict created by the dual command structure.

HUMAN PROBLEMS IN MATRIX ORGANIZATIONS

According to a study by Reeser (1969), there are several sets of human problems associated with matrix or project forms of organizations. Most of these problems center around anxiety concerning the temporariness of the situation and the need to report to two different bosses. Specific findings from the study are summarized here:

1. Personnel connected with project forms of organization suffer more anxieties about possible loss of employment than members of functional organizations. It seems that the temporary nature of projects creates personnel problems, particularly as the project comes to a close and people wonder if they will find a job on another project. If the organization has a history of always reassigning people, this problem can be lessened. If the employees do not trust the management, this problem is heightened.

2. Individuals temporarily assigned to matrix organizations are more frustrated by authority ambiguity than are permanent members of functional organizations. When individuals are first assigned to a matrix form of organization, they often find the dual reporting system to be frustrating. The functional form of organization emphasizes unity of command. The matrix form violates this principle.

3. Without unity of command, confusion and ambiguity are common conditions. This occurs because the jobs in the organization are often not clearly defined, authority relationships are obscure, and lines of communication are loose and unorganized. People connected with project forms of organization feel more frustrated because of lack of formal procedures and role definitions than do members of functional organizations.

4. The work environment in a project form of organization is often one of intense competition with other organizations for resources, recognition, and rewards. This leads to conflict, and frustrations caused by conflict are perceived more seriously by personnel connected with project forms of organization than by members of functional organizations.

Davis and Lawrence (1978) found similar problems in their diagnosis of matrix organizations. They point out that the essence of a matrix is dual command, so for such a form to survive, there needs to be a balance of power between the project managers and the department managers. This is not normally the case, particularly in organizations that evolved from a functional form. Matrix managers have to recognize that conflict is inherent in the matrix design. Conflict is not always detrimental since many creative ideas emerge from constructive conflict. The matrix system relies on worthy adversaries, counterparts who can match each other and turn the conflict to constructive ends.

SUMMARY

As indicated in this chapter, the matrix form of organization is not a panacea for the problems of the project manager. Like any organizational form, matrix seems to alleviate some types of problems while exacerbating others. So while the form helps to make the organization more responsive to changes in the environment, it seems to increase employee frustration and heighten some organizational power plays.

The complete project manager does not necessarily need a matrix organization. However, the complete project manager should understand what a matrix organization attempts to achieve. To foster this understanding has been the intent of this chapter.

In addition, the complete project manager understands how people experience matrix organization. The end-of-chapter reading (Stuntz, 1983), giving one person's experience in a matrix, is directed at providing a basis for such understanding.

REFERENCES

Bedeian, A. G. *Organizations: Theory and Analysis*. New York: The Dryden Press, 1984.

Davis, S. M. *Managing and Organizing Multinational Corporations*. New York: Pergamon Press, 1979.

Davis, S. M. and Lawrence, P. R. *Matrix*. Reading, Mass.: Addison Wesley, 1977.

Davis, S. M. and Lawrence, P. R. "Problems of Matrix Organizations," *Harvard Business Review*, 131–142, May–June 1978.

Dunne, E. J., Stahl, M. J., and Melhart, L. J. "Influence Scores of Project and Functional Managers in Matrix Organizations," *Academy of Management Journal*, 21:135–140, 1978.

Graham, G. H. *Understanding Human Relations: The Individual, Organization and Management*. Chicago, Ill.: Science Research Associates, 1982.

Kolodny, H. F. "Matrix Organization Designs and New Product Success," *Research Management,* 23:(5):29–33, 1980.

Price, J. L. "The Impact of Departmentalization on Interoccupational Cooperation," *Human Organization,* 27 362–368, 1968.

Reeser, C. "Some Potential Human Problems of the Project Form of Organization," *Academy of Management Journal,* 459–467, December 1969.

Stuntz, J. W. "A General Manager Talks about Matrix Management," in *Project Management Handbook* (D. Cleland and W. King, Eds.). New York: Van Nostrand Reinhold, 1983.

A GENERAL MANAGER TALKS ABOUT MATRIX MANAGEMENT*

John W. Stuntz

Influencing the Matrix with Financial Policies

How does the GM use financial management policies to influence the performance of a matrix-organized division? I could write a book, but a few paragraphs should suffice!

Probably the biggest matrix management problem is clear assignment of *accountability.* (That sentence probably should be printed in red!) This is the Siamese twin of the shared responsibility that is a primary characteristic of the matrix. But if performance can be measured, accountability can be assigned! As just described, it is easy to measure the program manager and hold him or her accountable. In fact, the manager's financial statement is a more explicit scorecard than the one the GM lives and dies by, because the business the PM manages is more precisely defined and bounded—it has a beginning and an end! The more challenging task is assignment of accountability to the functional managers, especially the middle tiers. If they are measured only by budget statements, their accountability for project performance will be poor or nonexistent. Summary statements of performance on project work packages, as described previously, are a big step forward.

A corollary situation has been observed. Suppose there is an organizational element that (1) runs programs on which it is measured, (2) manages budgets that are also measured, and (3) works on an array of assigned work package tasks on which, for reasons of organizational or financial statement inadequacy, it is not measured. What would be your estimate of that organization unit's performance in each of those categories? (One observer

---

*From *Matrix Management Systems* Handbook, edited by David I. Cleland. © Van Nostrand Reinhold, 1984.

has referred to that situation as being a wholesaler and a retailer simultaneously.) There are no walls thicker than paper walls. Financial statements that reward parochial behavior do not similarly credit service rendered to associates will isolate the elements and destroy the teamwork in a matrix, despite the most eloquent exhortations of the general manager—who is the ultimate victim. The best solution is accountability, measured at each functional cell, for all programs served by that cell.

A special organizational issue illustrates this point dramatically, while also raising additional issues. In the late 1960s, to accommodate growth and give more management attention to a historically neglected business segment, the product support business was segregated, with its own management, facilities, and business statements. The products it was supporting (with spares, test equipment, technical manuals, O & M training, and field tech reps) generally were the products we .were manufacturing. So the support business really derived from the product division's strategic investment and start-up risks. Additionally, many of the spares that the support organization sold were built concurrently on the same production line as the prime equipment. From the beginning, the shared strategic benefit was recognized by spreading the burden of strategic expenses equally on both statements. But with independent business statements, new parochial interest showed up, and it became an increasing struggle to get spares out of a shop that was measured on its performance in shipping prime equipment! And heated debates arose on allocation of contract funds to compensate for the "unfair" skewing of risks!

The solution to the matrix management problems raised here—and they were matrix problems, since they arose out of an arrangement involving shared responsibilities—was introduction of financial statements sometimes referred to as "matrix bookkeeping." Very simply, where there is shared responsibility, both get credit. This is easy to do. If the financial data system already collects costs by program and includes normal work breakdown structure detail, identification and summing of common parts is straightforward. (When the statements are aggregated for reporting up the corporate chain, it is equally routine to subtract the common parts so they won't be counted twice.)

Note the benefits of matrix bookkeeping. First, it eliminated that wholesaler-retailer inequity on the spares manufacturing (and spares shipments *did* pick up, dramatically, when we introduced the approach!). Second, it blunted the "zero-sum game" associated with the assignment of contract dollars.

Zero-sum games constitute a cancer endemic to matrix organizations. The resources are shared, they are finite, and "the more I get, the less you have." Success or failure usually depends on quality and quantity of resources applied. When financial statements clearly segregate and measure the degree of success and failure on a segment of the business, but prorate the cost of resources on some basis that does not truly reflect the degree of their utilization on the business segment so measured (and there is no practical way to accomplish that totally), then you have a zero-sum game. And the general manager referees all zero-sum games. To eliminate zero-sum games in the interest of teamwork instead of internal competition for the resources, the financial policies and procedures of the division should be designed to measure specifically what each manager is to be held accountable for.

THE PEOPLE DIMENSION

Organizations are arrangements of people. It has been said that a chief executive sets goals, selects people, and motivates the people to reach the goals—that's all—and two out of those three tasks relate to the "people" dimension.

A matrix is hard on people; most seem to find it so. In a recent employee-attitude survey at a large industrial complex that was matrixed (or whatever the verb is!) 15 to 20 years ago, the matrix organization drew the least favorable reaction in the whole survey. Analysis of the responses showed that the reaction was pretty much shared by all levels. The concerns were mostly personal, rather than objective: what happens to me and my career, what team do I belong to, how do I identify with the goals and successes of the enterprise, how can I serve multiple masters, does anybody really know whether I'm doing a good job? Partly these concerns are geared to "bigness," but the people mostly ascribe them to the matrix and its inherent ambiguities (as do I). So it becomes top priority for the general manager, *especially* the GM of a matrix organization, to understand and address at least the following three issues in the people dimension:

- Selection and training of management
- Conflict, trust, and motivation
- Creating a culture

Selection and Training of Management

Some managers will never adapt. If their personal style is authoritarian, the frustration of seldom having complete authority, of having to persuade a peer (worse, *yield* to him!) as a normal day-in, day-out operating mode, can make such individuals almost totally ineffective.

Such frustration at high level tends to be cancerous, infecting peers and subordinates more pervasively and more destructively than in simpler, more segregated organizational styles. A decision to convert to a matrix, therefore, must be based on an assessment of the available management team, and must allow for a transition period sufficient to gradually replace those who can't adapt to the traumatic change. (A good early retirement policy is a great asset for conversion to a matrix!) How about the GM himself? (Or herself?) *He* can be authoritarian; in fact, in a matrix organization at times it would actually help.

Some lower management levels have the mirror image of the lifelong autocrat's problem. At the intersections of the matrix there are two-boss managers, such as the engineering manager on program X, who reports to the program manager and also to the division engineering manager. Some can't live with that. (I often relate the story of such a man who came into my office in despair, complaining, "How can I work for two bosses?" I asked him if he was married. He suddenly realized he had *three!* I reminded him that we are born with two: that old one-boss catechism is a myth.) Actually some of us, when we were very young, learned how to use the *two* bosses to good advantage—a technique that extrapolates very well to the two-boss matrix situation.

How about retraining? That always helps as a tool to induce change. There are two kinds of training: one is substantive, to impart knowledge or skills; the other is behavioral, to change attitudes and style. The second, in my opinion, is nearly worthless. The first is invaluable, maybe essential. One of the best features of this "how to" training is that it demands that substantive "how to's" be generated, documented, standardized, communicated, and disciplined. The matrix is loose, flexible, dynamic; it requires much more interaction, dialogue, and decision making across organization unit boundaries—shared responsibilities for people as well as for technology and finance. As a consequence, there is a much greater need for formal, disciplined management systems, and that, of course, is the substance of those substantive training programs.

Creation of clear, comprehensive management systems for the control of finance, tasks, and people will have far-reaching benefits, including illumination of architectural soft spots in the organization itself, where a little "fine tuning" of the matrix would facilitate a better procedure. Take the case of those high-level program managers and functional managers who were described earlier as frustrated by their loss of authority. A carefully tuned organization, with sensitively balanced management systems and procedures, can clarify the mutual needs of the two matrix dimensions, thereby equitably balancing the power and authority that the two hierarchies must share. The natural balance will eliminate more frustration than will the training!

But the biggest beneficiaries of disciplined management systems are the people—all the people. Most of the concerns that showed up in that attitude survey were traceable either to the lack of clear, consistent management systems and rules, or to structural ambiguities that would have been revealed in the process of the management system generation.

The giant IBM may be the world's largest matrix (although they don't seem to use that term). In fact, theirs (like most) is a multidimensional matrix. At IBM many of the pieces come together only at the very top of the corporation; others tie together at the level of a site manager; while still others are in between, with several sites sharing responsibilities for meeting business, program, or functional goals. Significantly, IBM has a very comprehensive management system for dealing with all aspects of the management task—documented, thoroughly taught, followed with consistency and discipline. It's a case in point!

Let us return to the subject of training, because there's another side to that coin. The matrix provides a new opportunity for training and development of potential GMs. Historically, the step from functional management to general management has been very difficult. One reason is the need for understanding of multiple functions. A second may be the unforgiving nature of the GM's job, the performance of which is measured regularly by a numerical scorecard. As noted earlier, the program manager's job contains both of those same ingredients. But since programs come in all sizes, it is possible to both screen and train future general managers via the program management hierarchy just as, traditionally, we have been able to develop functional managers up through their organizational tiers. Eight of the last 12 general manager appointees in our long-time matrix organization have had substantial experience (successful, obviously!) as program managers. As a by-product, think how that trend affects the motivation and influence of program managers! Positive motivation is indeed required: their job may be even more hazardous than the GM's, since the program manager is on stage playing a one-string fiddle. Without some understanding from top management, there won't be many volunteers!

Conflict, Trust, and Motivation

In any organization the actions of top management largely determine the motivation of the entire assemblage. Body language transmits unmistakable messages, just as that pattern of GM appointments did. Take the case of conflict management. As noted before, a system of shared responsibilities (the matrix) not only is a conflict generator but, given the two communication paths, it is highly likely that an abundance of these conflicts will land in the GM's lap. At that point the GM can follow one of three courses, two of which would be demotivating (perhaps demoralizing) to the troops.

Hopefully the conflicts will be resolved in a timely fashion and in a manner that is interpreted to be based on merit, not personalities. The two bad alternatives would be (1) to leave them unresolved, which would lead to frustrating delays and probably a lot of ante-room in-fighting, or (2) to destroy the bearer of these bad tidings of conflict in the ranks (a technique that goes back at least to the ancient Greeks), which would isolate the front office for all time.

How do the program managers motivate the people they depend on for project success? They don't *own* them: let them try to order them around and see how far they get! (Actually, that limitation really is not unique to matrix organizations in modern high technology industry. Good engineers are as free as a bird! Too heavy a hand will send them to a competitor, probably for a 10% raise.) Unequipped to *drive* the project team, the program manager must lead them, which can only be done if they want to follow. And why would they want to follow? Well, this isn't a psychology text, but for most of us who have more than enough of worldly goods, the biggest motivators are our own personal pride in our accomplishments, a feeling of being a part of a team whose accomplishments we share, and—perhaps most rewarding—the respect and approval of associates whom we respect. We follow a person's leadership because we respect and trust that person, feel good about our mutual involvement with him or her and our associates in this team effort. The key words are respect, trust, mutual, team. Respect and trust almost have to be mutual: that's the way teams are built.

How do we give individuals in a very large matrix organization this sense of mutual respect and trust, of recognition for their individual contributions, of team identity and the relation of that team's effort to the larger organizational goals? Today's buzz word is "participative management." Sometimes called "Theory Z," it's not so much a fad as a necessity in the industrial ambiance just described. There are many techniques of participative management:

- A management open-door policy (even for the bearers of conflicts, and maybe especially for them)
- Management round tables
- Quality Circles
- Management's frequent presence "on the floor," listening more than talking
- A variety of formal "dialogue" programs

But the difference between a participative management program and true participative management has to do with the body language, the actions, the building of mutual respect and trust, emanating from the top. Trust starts with understanding. Given the inherently confusing nature of a big matrix, there is a need to publish explicit, meticulous organization charts, mission statements, and unit goals. And these must be explained and updated frequently. Groups within these organizations need to be recognized publicly for excellent performance in meeting their goals. And the individuals—particularly the individuals—should understand how they fit into one of these groups, and be recognized for superior contribution. In this regard, there may be no more important management institution than a credible individual "performance management system." Such a system can be the basis for a mutual understanding, between the individual and his or her boss *or bosses,* of the individual's personal performance objectives and accomplishments. It can be the basis for more credible—hence more positively motivating—recognition programs, merit increases, and promotion.

Creating a Culture

Some management scholars have asserted that matrix management is more a culture than an organizational structure. Cultures have to do with behavioral norms. A matrix can be created by the stroke of a pen, as it were, by laying out an organization (though there are layers of nuances there), by promulgating a manual of procedures (most necessary, most challenging), and by appointing managers who have the adaptability to work in this trying milieu. Real lasting success, however, depends on teamwork in a framework that makes teams hard to identify. Success depends on the *absence* of parochialism—a state that awaits nirvana! These are revolutionary cultural norms. They depend on the general manager who is at once the integrator of the loose structure and the behavioral style-setter. Meeting these demands, establishing the culture, may be his biggest challenge.

SUMMARY

At the beginning of this chapter the claim was made that general managers like the matrix. In the intervening pages we have noted that there is a lot for them to like:

- Efficient use of resources
- Technology transfusion that works
- Project performance measurement that is explicit and precise
- Focused customer attention
- Great general management development

However, nothing is free, and certainly not the matrix. Some of the costs include:

- A higher manager/employee ratio
- Diluted management control
- Motivational problems
- Complex management challenges

Also, the matrix places special demands on the general manager, who must be integrator, referee, and culture leader.

But the bottom line is that matrix management—structure, discipline, or culture—is being used, in one or another of its almost limitless forms, by most successful companies in the high-technology systems business. It's working, helping talented people to create more useful high-technology products, generating more profits for the investor. GMs, please note!

9
Managing for Creativity

One doesn't discover new lands without
consenting to lose sight of the shore
for a very long time.
André Gide, *The Counterfeiters*

This chapter is concerned with managing those projects in which the main product is creative thinking. It is not about managing creative groups or research and development groups in particular but rather about managing for creativity in general.

The chapter begins with a review of some general ideas about creativity as a process of innovation. The inner conditions and motivations for creativity are then discussed.

Throughout the chapter it is assumed that most people have the ability for creativity but most organizations do not foster this ability. The needs of the organization are then compared to the conditions for creativity.

Suggestions for creative management are also given. These suggestions come from discussions with managers of creative groups.

CREATIVITY

Creativity is normally thought to be a process of rearranging ideas or products to produce a new idea or product that is generally considered to be an innovation. Although the innovation is considered to be new, it is usually not the result of entirely new thinking or completely new ideas. Most innovations are the result of rearranging the relationship between or among ideas or products that are already in currency.

Adding or subtracting a part of an existing idea or product is not considered to be an innovation.

As an example of such ideas, consider the creation of the locomotive. The first railroads were used to haul coal from the coal mines to the ships in port. These railroads were drawn by horses. The steam engine was created to pump water out of the coal mines. Each of these products existed independently (i.e., there was no direct relationship between them) until someone applied some creativity and combined the products to form the first locomotive. Thus the innovation of the locomotive was the result of rearranging the relationship between existing products to form a new product.

Most people writing about creativity seem to agree that it resides within the individual. Teams of people may be used to foster creative thinking, but it is in the mind of the individual that the rearranging of relationships takes place. In addition, it is generally agreed that almost all people are capable of some form of creativity and innovation. This ability seems to be innate in human beings. However, it is often not used or not shown because it is not nurtured, encouraged, or rewarded. Thus it seems that the simple key to managing for creativity is the nurturing, encouraging, and rewarding of creativity in individuals.

This premise is generally much easier to state than to accomplish. The survival of organizations usually depends on innovations. Yet, almost paradoxically, the need for stability and conformity in these same organizations often acts to inhibit the very creativity that is required for survival. This paradox will be explored by first examining the conditions needed for creativity and then examining the conditions of most organizational functioning. With this understanding, we can then derive a model for managing for creativity.

Conditions for Creativity

Rogers (1970) laments that there is a dearth of creativity due to societal and cultural emphasis on conformity. To be original or different is often felt to be "dangerous." It is true, however, that organizations need rules for conformity in order that people may interact effectively. A constant change in the rules could indeed be dangerous to the existence of the organization. The problem as Rogers sees it, however, is that adherence to the rules in one area of organization is allowed to affect all areas of organization. Creativity has its place.

For the creative process, there must be some observable product of creation. Fantasies may be novel, but they cannot usefully be defined as creative unless they are symbolized in words, form, or deeds, or turned into an invention. Thus the end goal is seen as very important to the entire creative process. Managing for creativity is very much managing towards some end goal. Thus, network planning techniques that focus on project goals, and goal control techniques that focus on project execution, seem well suited to foster creativity.

The creative process is defined by Rogers (1970) as the "emergence in action of a novel relational product, growing out of the uniqueness of the individual on the one hand, and the materials, events, people, or circumstances of his life on the other." Thus creativity is part personal and part the materials of existence. This is why an innovation always has the stamp of the individual upon it—because each individual has his own way of seeing the world and his own experience of the materials of existence. Such unique views of the world are often not rewarded by the organization. Often, the leaders of the organization may wish all employees to view the world in some similar way.

The motivation to follow rules and procedures opposes the motivation for creativity. The motivation for creativity lies in man's tendency to actualize himself, to become his potentialities. This directional trend is evident in all organic and human life—the urge to expand, expend, develop, mature, and express and activate all the capacities of the organism. This tendency may be deeply buried under psychological defenses, but it is thought to exist in all people and to await only the proper conditions to be released and expressed.

Encouraging creativity is made more difficult because the resulting innovations are often impossible to judge. Frequently, the social (or organizational) value of a creative act cannot be determined by examining the product itself. In many cases, judgment must be suspended until the product comes into common usage. Simply because it is novel, we have no standards by which to judge it. It seems that the more original the product and the more far-reaching the consequences, the more it is judged as evil by contemporaries. Rogers (1970, p. 141) states, "It seems that no contemporary mortal can satisfactorily evaluate a creative product at the time it is formed, and this statement is increasingly true the greater the novelty of the creation."

So we see that creativity is both difficult to nurture and difficult to reward. It can, however, be managed. What is important to remember from this discussion is that people create because it is satisfying to them, it is self-actualizing. This is why many standard management techniques fail in the area of encouraging creativity. Creative people are marching to their own drummer and seeking their own deep-rooted rewards. They may not be seeking the rewards normally held out by managers in order to motivate people.

Inner Conditions of Constructive Creativity

At this point we examine some of the deep-rooted and inner conditions that seem to be necessary for creativity. Rogers (1970) has listed three of them as follows:

1. *Openness to experience—extensionality.* Openness to experience involves an awareness of the here and now rather than a constant emphasis on the future. It means a lack of rigidity in concepts, beliefs, perceptions, and hypotheses. It means a tolerance for ambiguity where ambiguity exists rather than trying to force closure onto a situation. It is often called the existential orientation.
2. *An internal locus of evaluation.* The value of the product is established not by the praise or criticism of others but by the creator. The person asks, "Have I created something that is satisfying to *me*?" This does not mean that the person is oblivious to external evaluation. It just means that the chief basis for evaluation lies inside the person rather than outside that person.
3. *Ability to toy with elements and concepts.* A creative person has the ability to juggle elements into impossible juxtapositions, to translate from one form to another, to state wild hypotheses, and to express the ridiculous. It is from this toying that there arises the hunch, the creative way of seeing life in a new and significant way.

The Creative Act and Its Concomitants

When the preceding conditions have been met, then creativity can occur. There seem to be several concomitants of creativity and innovation.

The first is what is called the *eureka* feeling: "This is IT. I have discovered IT. This is what I want to express."

The second is the anxiety of separateness. Rogers (1970) states this idea when he says, "I do not believe that any significant creative products are formed without the feeling, 'I am alone. No one has ever done just this before. I have ventured into territory where no one has been. Perhaps I am foolish, or wrong, or lost, or abnormal.' "

The third concomitant is the desire to communicate with a group that will understand. This is an enormously freeing experience—to communicate with people who think that your ideas have some merit or at least are not ridiculous. It is doubtful that a human being can create without wishing to share his creation. Almost by definition, the majority of people in the world will not share this vision. The creator will want to find a group with which he can share his innovation.

Conditions Fostering Creativity

Rogers summarizes conditions that foster creativity. He emphasizes that creativity cannot be forced, it must be permitted to emerge. This is best done under conditions of psychological safety (X) and psychological freedom (Y). The conditions are:

X1   Accepting the individual as of unconditional worth. This amounts to unconditional faith in a person, no matter what his present state. When a person senses this they feel a climate of safety. In this climate he can experiment, actualize himself in new and spontaneous ways—he is moving towards creativity.

X2   Providing a climate in which external evaluation is absent. For the individual to find himself in an atmosphere where he is not being evaluated, not being measured by some external standard, is enormously freeing. Evaluation is always a threat, always creates a need for defensiveness, always means that some portion of experience must be denied to awareness.

[I believe this will be the most difficult part in the management of creative groups. External evaluation is usually provided by the organization and/or the client. Almost by definition, management means evaluation. In theory, one is free to say, "I do not like your idea" because this is a reaction rather than an evaluation. However, the evaluation is often implied by the receiver, i.e., the sender does not like the idea because it is bad.]

X3   Understanding empathically. See the other person from their point of view and accept them.

Y   Psychological freedom. This is when the facilitating person [the manager] permits complete freedom of symbolic expression. Real expression such as anger is normally repressed by society. However, we can allow anger at a symbol. The permission is to be free, which also means that one is responsible—that is, the person is free to bear the consequences of his mistakes as well as his achievements.

THE INDIVIDUAL AND THE ORGANIZATION

The preceding discussion indicated some of the aspects of the creative process and the creative individual. In examining the problems of creativity in organizations, we have assumed that the needs of the creative individual are somewhat incongruous with the needs of the formal organization.

To examine this aspect of creativity in organizations, we use the conclusions of a paper written by Argyris (1957) on the needs of the individual and the organization: the assumed needs of the individual are reviewed first; the impact of some standard management concepts is reviewed next; then some conclusions, in the form of hypotheses, are listed.

The trends in individual development are:

1. From a state of being passive to a state of increasing activity.
2. From a state of dependence upon others to a state of relative independence. Relative independence is the ability to "stand on one's own two feet" and simultaneously recognize healthy dependencies.
3. From being capable of behaving in only a few ways to being capable of behaving in many different ways as an adult.

4. From having erratic, shallow, quickly dropped interests to possessing a deepening of interests.
5. From a short time perspective to having a much longer time perspective.
6. From being in a subordinate position to aspiring to occupy at least an equal and/or superordinate position relative to peers.
7. From having lack of awareness of self to having an awareness of, and control over, the self as an adult. The adult who experiences adequate and successful control over his own behavior develops a sense of integrity and feelings of self-worth.

The basic principles of organization seems to go against these tendencies of individual growth. The following material provides some examples.

Task Specialization.   Task specialization ignores the tendency towards self-actualization and requires an individual to use only a few of his abilities. This also causes whatever little skill is left in the job to become enormously important—small differences in ability make large differences in output. What you can do is more important than who you are.

Chain of Command.   With the chain-of-command assumption of organizations, the primary responsibility of management is to control, direct, and coordinate the interrelationships of the parts and to make certain that each part performs its objective. It is further assumed that the top can direct and control the part on the bottom. If the parts are individuals, they must be motivated to accept this direction, control, and coordination of their behavior. This makes the individuals dependent upon, passive, and subordinate to the leader. It also shortens time perspective because they do not control the information necessary to predict their futures. With this dependency, there seems little chance that a person will act creatively.

Unity of Direction.   Here the leader sets the goals. Individual growth requires that individuals be able to set their own goals. Often, goals are set in a vacuum such that the goals of the individual are in conflict with the goals of the organization. This may be necessary for some jobs, but it is not conducive to individual growth or creativity.

For creative management, the two sets of goals should be determined together.

Span of Control.   Low span of control usually results in an individual having less control over his work situation. This will increase his feelings of dependence, submissiveness, passivity, etc.

Effect on the Individual.   These seemingly inherent aspects of the formal organization have a profound effect on the individual, particularly in the areas of stimulating innovation. Argyris (1957) concludes his argument with the following scenario of the problems brought on by the needs of formal organization.

1. There is a lack of congruency between the needs of healthy individuals and the demands of the formal organization. This will create a disturbance which is in proportion to the degree of incongruency.
2. The results of the disturbance are frustration, failure, short time perspective, and conflict.
3. The nature of formal principles causes the subordinate, at any given level, to experience competition, rivalry, and intersubordinate hostility and to develop a focus towards the parts rather than the whole.
4. This is a circular process. Dependence results in a "parts" orientation, which causes more dependence, which shows the need for more management, which leads to more dependence, etc.
5. Employees react to all this by such things as leaving, being psychologically defensive (daydreaming, aggression, ambivalence, regression, projection, etc.), becoming apathetic towards the organization and its goals, creating informal groups, and stressing the nonhuman or material factors.
6. Managers react to this by increasing (1) the degree of their pressure-oriented leadership, (2) the degree of the use of management controls, and/or (3) the number of "pseudo"-participation and communications programs.
7. Such an action-reaction pair tends to compound the problem—it increases dependence and subordination, which increases the employees' adaptive behavior that management was trying to

curtail, which increases management reaction, etc. The basic problem is to reduce the degree of dependency, subordination, submissiveness.

DEVELOPMENT OF CREATIVE MANAGEMENT MODELS

Much of the history of management thinking has been along the lines of prescribing, directing, and controlling. Much of this past thinking stemmed from studying the advances in output that were achieved during the industrial revolution. For those advances, specialization was the key. Only the manager knew the total process, and he directed each specialist to do merely a part while he controlled the whole. So the model for direction and control was:

Along this line, we get the classic management functions that are usually given as plan, organize, direct, staff, and control.

One of the assumptions for the case of creative groups is that the managers may not know the total process or the end product. If this is the case, then management becomes more of a support function than a directional function. So in this case, the model for direction and control/support could be given as

With this model, managers often feel that they are powering a rudderless ship. With the first model there seems to be too much direction and control to stimulate creativity, while with the second model all direction and control seem to be missing. The ideal probably lies somewhere in between.

The middle ground here is generally called the sandwich model which looks like the following:

With this model, the manager both directs and supports in such a way as to help develop a climate for maximum creativity. Given these assumptions, we can now examine each of the classical management functions and see how they relate to the problems of managing for creativity.

Plan and Organize

Managers, through the use of their authority, will normally plan the work and organize the tasks to be done by their subordinates. Completing this managerial task involves the assumption that the process for creating the final product is known to the manager. For the work of creative groups, the final product is normally not known in advance; therefore, the assumptions of planning and organization are not necessarily valid in this case.

One of the assumptions of planning is that it is necessary for everyone to be heading in the same direction. It assumed that the plan is to provide the "goal" towards which everyone is supposed to be heading. The basic assumption is that there must be some sort of "psychic unity" of the group in order to foster group cohesion and performance. This is supposedly achieved through a commonality of motives. However, as argued in Chapter 5, some people feel that psychic unity is not necessary for group performance. What is necessary for group performance is the ability to understand each other's behavior, to get to know one another. In this context, the function of planning and control is to create a climate for group cohesion rather than to make sure that all are headed in the same direction. In fact, in creative processes one does not necessarily want all people headed in the same direction. Many creative ideas are created when people head off in several different directions.

Direct

Given the plan and organization, the managers must now direct the workers as to what they should do in order to realize the goal in the plan. There are many assumptions here involving the "man as automaton" theme, namely, that people can be used merely as passive tools in the organizational machinery. These assumptions may work on production lines and other fixed production systems (so-called mechanistic systems). However, it is doubtful that creative processes will flourish under strict direction.

For the creative process, the manager cannot, indeed should not, direct the work. Telling someone "how to do it" negates his value as a human being and does not allow for growth or creative expression. What you are looking for in creative work is a new combination of previously existing ideas. This new combination cannot be directed but can be "supported."

Staff

Staffing considerations often have to do with numbers: How many people do we need to do this job? From this consideration, we get a whole set of concepts having to do with efficiency. There is a history of time and motion studies, scientific management, and the like. The root of all of these lies in repeatable tasks, which are not the stuff of creative groups. Staffing creative groups requires turning away from an input orientation towards an output orientation—from Theory X to Theory Y—and turning from efficiency towards synergy.

An input orientation again assumes that we know the process and the result. If we know these, we can direct people and be aware of how many people we need in order to complete the product. We assume that if the right number of people are put in the right amount of hours, then the product will emerge. This orientation fosters a concentration on input rather than output, particularly since the output is known and the input is unknown.

It is indeed true that the results of creative groups derive from the fruitful interaction of people. These results correlate somewhat with the time spent working on a problem and with the number of people in the group—but not necessarily. Thus the more important staffing considerations become who is in the group and how group members interact, instead of how many people are needed for a particular job.

Control

Control is normally associated with measurement, usually financial. Three ideas seem pertinent here. The first is that control should be designed to buffer against external interference. The second is a results orientation. The third is that creative people will find creative ways around any control system that they consider oppressive, so the system should be designed with creative people in mind.

The first idea about control involves the question of what you are trying to control and why. An internal orientation to control is to set up for control of expenditures. An external orientation is to control outside interference. Creative groups need to be protected, not harassed. Some control over expenditures is naturally important in any organization. However, constant and overt concentration on expenditures can limit creative potential. One of the stimulations to creativity is the ability to take risks, to have a go and think boldly. The control system should somehow encourage this if creativity is indeed desired. One should be rewarded, not punished, for taking risks. Applying well-known, tried and trusted general accounting principles for control may make good accounting sense but may also be counter-creative. Some creative thought is needed in the design of control systems to foster creativity.

The second consideration is that the control system should mirror the creative process, as discussed in Chapter 2. This process normally has what is seen as a slow start-up period—a period of incubation. During this time, the amount of visible activity or product may be low. This low output activity builds to a critical point, a point where the due date or "the wall" is in sight. Sometimes people try to move the wall. If this cannot be done, then there is a sudden—or so it seems —burst of often frenzied activity as people work up to the last minute in order to deliver the product by the deadline. Once the product has been created, there is need for a relaxation period before starting again.

The problem with most control systems is that they seem to favor expenditure streams that are even and smooth. Such rates of expenditure are obviously easier to control. It often happens that the control system begins to dictate expectations so that people begin to expect a smooth stream of expenditure and results. Such is not the case for creative groups, and one should not allow the control system to dictate expectations.

Designing a control system to mirror the creative process may seem idealistic. However, people get around whatever system is in place anyway. Therefore, it seems that we should study the way people do cope with such systems in order to realize some alternative design principles. In the end, it appears that there will be a move towards a team design process to create the system. The manager is important here because there are outside forces such as banks whose needs must be met in order for the organization to remain viable. The manager thus takes on a boundary spanning role for this function, satisfying the bank but protecting his people from its interference.

Summary of Creativity and Organizations

For management of creativity, some of the classical management functions need to be reinterpreted. Planning and organizing should stress group development, as well as specifying the end goal and process. Directing should be more supportive. Staffing considerations should emphasize synergy rather than efficiency. Controls should be protective and should mirror the creative process. This does not mean that all of the standard management tools ought to be ignored. It does suggest that a part of the emphasis should be shifted. Thus, the manager needs to be both directive and supportive at the same time, or directive at some times and supportive at others. The trick for managers is to figure out when to be directive and when to be supportive.

The management model that seems to be suggested from this discussion is something like the sandwich model shown here:

This model indicates that the manager directs the worker from above while supporting the worker from below. This implies that the manager would work with employees to determine the direction and the goals, as well as the design control systems which support the creativity needed to reach those goals.

SUGGESTIONS FROM MANAGERS OF CREATIVE GROUPS

The sandwich model for managing for creativity was derivd from a consideration of the creative process, the motivations for creativity, and management practices that might inhibit creativity. The model and the suggestions for improving management for creativity were then reviewed by managers of creative groups in order to get their suggestions.

From discussions with managers of creative groups, the following ideas seemed to emerge:

1. Instead of communicating an end product or goal, what needs to be communicated is a VISION. Specifying a final product may imply a process, it may restrict imagination, and it may inhibit creative interaction. An overall and wide-reaching vision would act as the idea that compels people to action. This becomes the top part of the management "sandwich" model. The manager must continually communicate, refine, and re-communicate the vision.

2. Creative people are not special, unmanageable, etc. The characteristics which are normally associated with creative people are the same for all people. The difference is that in managing creative groups, you are asking people to be creative. This is usually not the case in production-type enterprises. An example

cited was the case of a bank teller. In such a case, the manager usually does not want the teller to be creative about the way he cashes a check. In this case, the product is known and the procedure is specified. Such is not the case in creative processes.

Creative groups may be different because the personality processes of people who choose to work in these groups differ from those of people who choose to work in other types of groups. For example, it was assumed that all people want recognition, but people who work in creative groups may want more recognition than others. However, it was also assumed that when people are asked to be creative, they seek recognition through the final product of their work.

3. When the end product and process are not specified, people want to "do it right," which can be interpreted to mean "do it their way." The facilities to do it right need to be supplied by the managers. Facilities for communicating with others constitute one example. Being protected from harassment by accountants is another.

4. People respond to controls on deadlines, usually. There is often a lot of rushing around at the last minute, but even this can be reduced by using some strict rules such as "I will not come in on the weekend." Although the last minute rush was often observed, people did not seem to think it was required.

5. Groups are important. All people need psychological homes. Competition between groups may inhibit the amount of information shared, but it increases the number of attempts to reach the vision.

6. Trust is paramount, in both directions. That is, the manager must trust the group and the group must trust the manager. The manager must be ready to take strange positions and to defend them against his peers who are using more conventional management. The manager must believe that people will respond positively to positive acts and must trust that people will not take advantage of his trust in them.

Trust is a large part of implementing an output orientation and moving to goal control. Once the vision has been communicated, and the necessary assets supplied to the employees, the manager must be ready to let go and show a trust that the work will be completed. The trust becomes self-fulfilling. If the manager can create an atmosphere of trust, then the employees will respond in a trustworthy manner. It's true. Trust me.

7. Creative management is the result of a conscious plan on the part of the manager to allow and encourage creativity. This requires that the manager have a good definition of what his job really entails. He can then pick out the parts that allow for creativity and encourage employees to behave accordingly. The manager must do this himself and not look to upper management to define the job or the creative parts of the job for him.

8. Question every rule and assumption. Many decisions are made or not made on the basis of long held rules of thumb or widely believed, but rarely tested, assumptions. Merely questioning the rules is a beginning of creativity, as is examining relationships. Once relationships have been examined, they could be changed, but if the old relationships are never questioned, new relationships may never be found.

9. Move from a mind-set of job security to individual security. Try to feel secure in being yourself, not in being in your current job. Concern with job security implies evaluation and control over YOU. Such concern is a well-known killer of creativity. When someone else sets the rules, it is usually for his own benefit and not necessarily for yours.

   Overconcern for job security implies an overconcern with someone else's evaluation of your work. This is contrary to the need for internal locus of evaluation and control in order to foster creativity. If you do this as a manager, your employees are likely to do the same thing, thus reducing their creative abilities.

10. Leadership is most effective in creating a vision and in boundary spanning activities. People enjoy a challenge, so the vision should be challenging. The more far-reaching and broader the vision, the more areas will people look into for ideas. Fly high in creating the vision because the manager who flies the highest sees the farthest.

    Relations with the rest of the organization constitute another area in which people will look to you for leadership. If the organization is allowed to constantly impose its value system on the group, creativity will be thwarted. Strong leadership is needed to combat the noncreative tendencies inherent in formal organizations.

11. A necessary ingredient to all this is a large amount of self-confidence. Life on the boundary is not easy as there are conflicting demands on both sides. The manager has to be able to let go, give control to others, and be responsible for the consequences. This responsibility will normally be to a group of people who do not understand, or have empathy for, the management style that encourages creativity.

What was not discussed with the managers was the ability of the project manager to do all this. It seems that the person needs to be very secure in his/her definition of self. The person must be able to let go of the reigns. The person must be vision and not task oriented. The person must be very good at boundary spanning because there will always be demands from the organization for the usual things such as stability, projections, fiscal responsibility, and the like. The manager has to be able to let the people do the work, to give them pride of ownership and the recognition that goes with success. The project manager must be a good change agent. A plan for change is thus presented in Chapter 10.

SUMMARY

The use of network techniques may appear to be overly structured to be useful for managing for creativity. However, the complete project manager is aware that techniques that structure thinking can be used to enhance creative thinking. This can be done by continually stressing the network as the path to the VISION. A well drawn network also helps to structure interactions by indicating relationships between activities. Finally, the network representation helps to stimulate creative left-brain thinking by showing all of the team members the "big picture."

REFERENCES

Argyris, C. "The Individual and the Organization: Some Problems of Mutual Adjustment," *Administrative Science Quarterly,* 1–24, 1957.
Rogers, C. R. "Towards a Theory of Creativity" in *Creativity* (P. E. Vernon, Ed.). Harmondsworth, England: Penguin Books, 1970.

THEORY Y ASSUMPTIONS IN A NON-THEORY Y WORLD*

Walter Nord

Washington University

Douglas McGregor's famous Theory *Y* and related behavioral science concepts have had a major impact on management and management education. Basically these approaches share a common set of assumptions which Tannenbaum and Davis [15] described as a shift:

Away from a view of man as essentially bad, to a view of him as basically good . . .

Away from avoidance or negative evaluation of individuals, toward confirming them as human beings . . .

Away from the view of individuals as fixed toward seeing them as processes . . .

Away from resisting the theory of individual differences toward accepting and utilizing them . . .

Away from utilizing an individual primarily with reference to the job description toward viewing him as a whole person . . .

Away from primary emphasis on competition toward a much greater emphasis on collaboration . . . (pp. 69–79).

For simplicity, I will refer to these models collectively as "theory *y*" approaches.

To say that "theory *y*" approaches have had a significant impact on management, does not necessarily mean that they are responsible for widespread changes in how organizations are *actually* run and how people are *actually* managed. While "theory *y*" approaches have had some impact on how organizations are managed, it appears they have affected more what managers feel or say they do (or ought to do), than what they actually do.

A somewhat paradoxical situation exists. Managers actively seek ways to manage their subordinates effectively. Academicians and consultants provide a fairly concise body of advice and an underlying rationale to meet this need. Organizations have devoted significant resources to introduce these concepts to their members and have acknowledged the value of these concepts publicly. However, the concepts have had little impact on how organizations are actually run. Why?

Elsewhere [10–12] I have explored in more detail why "theory *y*" concepts have not been applied more fully. While these reasons are complex, many of them can be boiled down to one basic deficiency—inadequate analysis of the nature of the worlds in which people and organizations function. Most "theory *y*" advocates are optimistic about human nature. They have assumed that models such as Maslow's hierarchy of needs provide valid descriptions of human nature. Furthermore, they are optimistic about the nature of the world. They have assumed that the type of environments which will bring forth the "higher levels" of human motivation either exist, are inevitable, or are easy to create. While their assumptions about human nature can be questioned, I believe the low impact of concepts is due more to the inadequacy of the "world assumptions" than to the models of human nature.

I am very willing to assume that there is a set of possible worlds in which humans would function at the higher levels of being. Unfortunately, when I compare the nature of these possible worlds with the current one, I find it difficult to believe that in the near future very many organizations will be operating in "theory *y*" worlds.

As I see it at least four necessary conditions must exist before organizational participants are apt to behave the ways described by Tannenbaum and Davis. First, the amount of non-zero sum conflict would be relatively great compared to the amount of conflict which *is* zero sum. Secondly, there would be a high degree of shared goals among individuals in operating units. Thirdly, either there would be no differences in power among individuals or there would be ways to neutralize the effects of inequalities of power among individuals. Finally, some mechanism would exist to eliminate the necessity for individuals to do routine work. For example, routine work could be eliminated by automation or we could subsidize inefficiencies caused by making such work less routine. Let's look at these conditions individually.

Non-zero sum conflict

Centuries ago Hobbes pointed out a certain problem faced by human societies—the war of each against all. Cooperative human efforts are still inhibited by the efforts of each individual to satisfy his/her interests in a world of scarce resources. Cooperative human efforts are plagued by conflict and limited to relatively unstable coalitions. By contrast, most of the "theory *y*" assumptions seem to be more consistent with situations where the struggle of each individual is relatively unimportant. "Good" as opposed to "bad" behavior, mutual human confirmation, acceptance of individual differences, and the emphasis on collaboration as opposed to competition are all more probable when people are not involved in struggles for scarce economic and social resources.

Resolution of conflict under these conditions is, of course, far easier than it is when people are in competition with each other for scarce resources. Under conditions of scarcity, the use of manipulative or morally questionable tactics as opposed to open, rational discourse are very normal human responses. Unfortunately, many fundamental processes in organizations stem from the competition for scarce resources.

Pfeffer [13] outlined many of these processes explicitly. He concluded:

"Our prescriptions are to recognize the inevitability of the political nature of resource-allocation decisions, the role of organizational mythology and techniques of legitimation in making the operation of power less obtrusive, and the fact that power accrues to those who control critical resources or who, either alone or through alliances with other internal or external groups, are capable of coping with critical organizational uncertainties. It is invariably the case that the use of power has observable consequences. More attention to the actual consequences of organizational decisions, and less concern with the mythology and rhetoric associated with the decision-making processes, will produce better insights into organizational functioning. (p. 262)."

It will be an interesting problem for historians to account for the fact that a significant body of management theory, based on the assumptions outlined by Tannenbaum and Davis, flourished simultaneously with Watergate, murder of a candidate for union office, shooting of political dissidents (e.g., Kent State), the overthrow of numerous top managers in corporations, the operation of Mayor Daly's and other political machines, the charges that slander of individual employees by members of one of the nation's largest utilities drove an executive to suicide, and so forth. If the characteristics of organizations are normally distributed, and even if the organizations which produced the results I've just listed are at the extreme end of one tail of the distribution (let alone near the mean), it is indeed not surprising that "theory y" concepts are not more widely applied.

Shared goals

A common correlate of the assumption of non-zero sum conflict is the assumption that people in organizations share common goals. Undoubtedly there are important shared goals (e.g., the survival of the organization). However, many organizations do not appear to be threatened by extinction in the foreseeable future. Consequently, often there is a pool of discretionary resources and substantial room for disagreement as to how this slack ought to be allocated.

To assume that consensus on the allocation of slack is similar to consensus on survival is unwarranted and probably false. Perhaps a useful analogy would be to consider a hierarchy of needs for organizations. Once the survival needs are met, a whole series of different processes and needs become more important. Such outcomes as fairness, service to constituents not directly related to survival, organizational prestige, interdepartmental status and other "higher" level criteria take on new importance. Many of these issues induce struggles among people who have quite divergent interests. Moreover, organizational participants are constantly competing for promotion, control of resources, and other outcomes which accrue to "successful" individuals.

Consequently, although shared goals exist, the degree to which they affect ongoing behavior in comparison to nonshared goals is problematic. The assumption that collaborative decision-making is a viable replacement for competition in such organizations is dubious. Strategies based on the assumption of shared goals, when important goals are not shared, are of limited utility.

Power inequalities

Few "theory *y*" adherents have questioned the need for hierarchical organization structures. However, it is by no means clear that such formal hierarchies and the resulting power inequalities, are compatible with values put forth by Tannenbaum and Davis. In fact, there is a growing body of evidence which suggests that inequalities in power are incompatible with so-called humanized social relationships.

Inequalities of power lead to several important outcomes. Kipnis [8] reported that possession of power induced people to behave coercively and to prefer to maintain psychological distance from their subordinates. Similarly Rosenhan [14] and Zimbardo [1] found that individuals who have rather absolute power over others (e.g., members of psychiatric staffs in mental hospitals and guards in a mock prison) treated the less powerful individuals in nonhumane ways.

The lack of power also has consequences for the less powerful individuals. Several writers (e.g., Harrington [6] and Gouldner [5]) have argued that the feeling of powerlessness can have damaging psychological consequences for the "powerless." On the other hand, when subordinates possess even potential power, the nature of the relationship changes. For example, the classic paper by Mechanic [9] revealed how prisoners in a maximum security prison commanded respect from the guards who realized that at some point their lives might depend on his relations with the prisoners.

In short, gross discrepancies in the relative power of individuals, which exist in most organizations, reduce likelihood that the "theory *y*" assumptions about human "goodness" will be consistent with the actual behavior of people in such organizations. Human nature, at least at its current state of evolution, seems to require relative equality in power if individuals are to treat each other with mutual respect and as whole persons, and to behave in ways which lead to mutual confirmation. Management theories and strategies which do not take this fact into account are unlikely to be useful, except as a source of platitudes.

Assumptions about work and technology

Underlying many of the "theory y" approaches are certain assumptions about the role of work in the lives of individuals and the nature of work and technology. First it is assumed that work is and ought to be a central life interest of individuals. There is, of course, a growing amount of evidence which counters this assumption (see Goldthorpe [4], Hulin and Blood [7], Fein [3]).

In addition, there are certain assumptions about work itself. It is commonly assumed that it is possible to provide an adequate number of jobs which use the "full potential" of individuals without sacrificing organizational effectiveness. However, organizations are under pressure to produce more goods at relatively low prices. Routine "core technologies" are frequently more consistent with achievement of this outcome than are the deroutinized ones envisioned by the theorists.

Those who base the feasibility of their change strategies on the deroutinization of work seem to have left several questions unanswered. Edmund Faltermayer [2] asked, "Who will do the dirty work tomorrow?" Second, how much slack are organizations willing to devote to these ends? Who are the advocates of this allocation within an organization—the stockholders? the CEO's? union leaders? the workers? Who stands to benefit from the introduction of such changes?

It appears that even lower-level participants, who are often thought to be prime beneficiaries of these changes, might prefer the slack to be given to them in higher wages or shorter work weeks as opposed to being devoted to making work more interesting and involving. How many people would prefer enriched jobs to, say, a 10% reduction in hours of work with no decrease in pay? Many people may prefer to have only peripheral involvement in work and to devote more time and energy to competing interests and demands. In fact, such preferences may be socially desirable. The Protestant Ethic notwithstanding, individuals who become workaholics are not necessarily more desirable socially than are individuals who work their 40 (or fewer) hours per week, and save most of their psychological and physical energy for non-work activities.

In sum, there do not appear to be enough influential advocates for the redesign of work according to "theory y" principles to stimulate the allocation of scarce resources to this goal. Individuals concerned with efficiency may not want to entail the risks. Individuals who would actually have to make the change may not fully know how to do it, and may not be willing to undergo the costs to do so. The individuals who supposedly benefit from such changes may prefer that the resources involved be devoted to different outcomes.

Conclusion

In many ways the values summarized by Tannenbaum and Davis are values I would like to promote. Moreover, I am not suggesting that these values are too idealistic to be achievable. I *am* suggesting that management strategies, that many behavioral scientists hope will support the acceptance of such values, are doomed to failure. This is because these strategies embody implicit assumptions about the nature of people and organizations which are incomplete and/or inaccurate. Assumptions about individuals, without comparable assumptions about the nature of their environments, do not provide a sound basis for effective action. The problem, as I see it, is to design social systems which support the values summarized by Tannenbaum and Davis. Psychological models alone will not provide an adequate foundation for such work. Rather, social, political, and economic changes are needed to encourage the development and survival of systems useful in the real world.

References

[1] Zimbardo., A Pirandellian Prison, *New York Times Magazine,* April 8, 1973, pp. 38–40, ff.–49.

[2] Faltermayer, E., Who Will Do the Dirty Work Tomorrow? *Fortune,* January, 1974, pp. 132–136.

[3] Fein, M., Motivation for Work. In R. Dubin (Ed.), *Handbook of Work, Organization, and Society,* Chicago: Rand McNally, 1976, pp. 465–530.

[4] Goldthorpe, J. H., Attitudes and Behavior of Car Assembly Workers: A Deviant Case and a Theoretical Critique, *British Journal of Sociology,* 1966, 17, pp. 227–244.

[5] Gouldner, A. W., *The Coming Crisis of Western Sociology,* New York: Basic Books, 1970.

[6] Harrington, M., *The Other America,* Baltimore: Penguin Books, 1962.

[7] Hulin, C. L. and Blood, M. R., Job Enlargement, Individual Differences, and Worker Responses, *Psychological Bulletin,* 1968, 69, pp. 41–55.

[8] Kipnis, D., Does Power Corrupt? *Journal of Personality and Social Psychology,* 1972, 24, 33–41.

[9] Mechanic, D., Sources of Power and Lower Participants in Complex Organizations, *Administrative Science Quarterly,* 1962, 7, pp. 349–364.

[10] Nord, W. R., The Failure of Current Applied Behavioral Science: A Marxian Perspective, *Journal of Applied Behavioral Science,* 1974, 10, pp. 557–578.

[11] ——, Economic and Socio-Cultural Barriers to Humanizing Organizations. In H. Meltzer and F. R. Wickert (Eds.), *Humanizing Organizational Behavior,* Springfield, Ill.: Charles C. Thomas, 1976, pp. 175–193.

[12] ——— and Durand, D. E., The Human Resources Approach and Organizational Realities: Some Neglected Issues, *Organizational Dynamics,* in press.

[13] Pfeffer, J., Power and Resource Allocation in Organizations. In B. M. Star and G. R. Salancik (Eds.), *New Directions in Organizational Behavior,* Chicago: St. Clair Press, 1977, pp. 235–265.

[14] Rosenhan, D. L., On Being Sane in Insane Places, *Science,* 1973, 179, pp. 250–258.

[15] Tannenbaum, R. and Davis, S. A., Values, Man, and Organizations, *Industrial Management Review,* 1969, 10, pp. 67–86.

10
Implementation of Project Management Techniques

It must be considered that there is nothing more difficult
to carry out, nor more doubtful of success, nor more dangerous
to handle, than to initiate a new order of things.
Niccolo Machiavelli, *The Prince,* 1513

This chapter is concerned with some of the behavioral aspects of implementing the project management techniques discussed in this book. The chapter begins with some general concepts of the problems associated with implementing change (as the opening quotation suggests, this is not particularly easy). From these general concepts, a model of change is presented.

Most studies show that change normally requires the push of a dedicated change agent. Thus some patterns of successful change agents are reviewed. It seems that the life of a change agent is very political, so the politics of implementation is another important topic. Finally, a 12-step implementation plan is suggested.

IMPLEMENTING CHANGE

In this book, I have attempted to illustrate how project managers could better manage projects by essentially working smarter and not necessarily harder. One manager, after reading parts of the manuscript, came to me and said that what I proposed did not seem like

*This chapter was coauthored with Dennis J. Cohen, Management and Behavioral Science Center, The Wharton School, University of Pennsylvania.

management to him. Although he liked many of the ideas, he did not see how he could possibly implement any of them in his organization. He did not think that these ideas would be accepted by many managers in his group, and he did not feel that he had the power to change the organization. As time passed, I found this to be a common reaction. Thus the purpose of this chapter is to discuss the acceptance of ideas, as well as power in organizations, so that project managers can devise a strategy for implementation. The chapter will be organized along these lines by first discussing the acceptance of ideas, then discussing the politics of implementation, and finally outlining a plan for developing a strategy of implementation.

Administrative Change

The type of change we are concerned with here generally comes under the heading of administrative change. This distinguishes it from the change involved in introducing a new invention such as the steam engine or the computer, although the administrative change might be based on a new invention. Administrative changes require modification in the way some of the organization's personnel carry out their daily work and are normally associated with the initiation of new procedures such as formal control systems and the use of PERT/CPM. Under this heading, we can also include general changes in the way people are treated, as in moving from Theory X-based procedures to Theory Y-based procedures.

Youker's (1983) article on implementing change in organizations indicates that "the history of the introduction of administrative systems changes is replete with failures." Such a statement certainly agrees with Machiavelli's feelings on change given in the opening quote, and neither statement bodes well for the potential change agent, the project manager.

There seem to constantly be studies of administrative systems, and all seem to recommend change. Some of the changes are never implemented, while others have a modest initial success and then die out over time. Some of the changes are unnecessary or ill advised, to be sure. However, the implementation rate of new procedures seems to be low even when there is a demonstrated benefit for the organization. For example, a study by Davis (1974) indicates that only 55% of the major construction firms in the United States were effectively using

CPM. Urban's (1974) study of management science models in general indicates that only about 3% of those models had ever really been implemented. Such numbers seem to say that implementing change is a next-to-impossible task.

One usual response to implementation problems is to point to people's so-called resistance to change. The person with the hot idea, at least from his viewpoint, might argue that people will not accept his idea because people just plain resist change. However, it should be abundantly clear that this is not true. Some change is readily accepted and quickly implemented. For example, within a relatively few years of its commercial introduction, a high percentage of U.S. homes adopted television. The xerographic copy machine was also quickly adopted and thus changed several aspects of current business practice. By this time, we wonder what we did without them. The desktop computer will probably follow the same development path.

So it would seem clear that resistance to change is not an innate human characteristic. In fact, the discussion of human growth in Chapter 9 would indicate that the opposite was true, that people innately desire to grow, to expand, and to become their potentialities. If we accept this assumption, then it seems clear that people will accept and even seek change if it helps them to grow and expand. One would also expect that a person would resist change if it does not help him to grow and expand. Finally, one can expect very severe resistance if the change restricts growth that has already taken place, that is, if the change seems to take something away.

The more general statement of this idea is that people will accept change that they perceive to be in their benefit and will resist change that they perceive not to be in their benefit. Lorsch (1974) summarizes his study of change with the idea that "the way persons respond to an attempt to change their behavior seems to depend on an implicit cost/benefit analysis which they make of the change."

From this argument, it seems clear that the key to understanding acceptance or resistance to change is people's *perception* of the benefits of the change. Often times a project manager will see the benefits of a change quite clearly, but the people around him will not perceive these benefits in the same way. It could be that what the project manager sees as a benefit, other people see as a detriment. In such a case, the gain of value to the project manager is seen as a loss of value to the others involved with the project. Thus the first step in a strategy to implement change is to be able to understand the effects of the change from the other person's point of view.

Dane et al. (1981) conducted a study on successfully introducing project management techniques into an organization. This study was only for one organization, but the results are similar to other studies and support theoretical models of change processes. In this study, nine factors were considered as possible explanations for the success or failure of implementation. The nine factors were:

1. Date of introduction
2. Rank of person making the introduction
3. Organizational scope of application
4. Length of planning horizon
5. Announced purpose for introducing PERT/CPM
6. Software awareness
7. Use of standardized format for network
8. Use of resource scheduling
9. Ability to do updating

The use of multiple regression analysis identified two factors which appeared to explain the successful introduction of PERT/CPM in the organization. These factors were the level of the person making the introduction and the stated purpose of the introduction. Both of these factors were found to be statistically significant at the 95% level of confidence.

Top management support is generally considered essential for introducing management science techniques into an organization. This finding appears in all studies that have been completed. The significance of this study was the inclusion of the statement of purpose. The statement of purpose gave a broad range of reasons for introducing the technique, including the effect the technique would have on the people involved. In this way, the people involved were given the information necessary to determine their own cost/benefit for the change. They apparently felt the change was of value to them since the implementation was successful. For many implementation efforts, however, such information is not provided and people begin to fear the worst. It thus seems clear that providing information about the personal effects of the change is another key to a successful implementation strategy.

A GENERAL MODEL OF CHANGE

The results from the study just cited agree well with a general model of adoption of innovations put forward by Wallace (1970). We will review that model at this point in order to gain further insight into how to develop a successful change strategy.

Wallace's model is based on the study of change agents attempting to introduce innovations to entire societies. For our purposes, the organization will be seen as a society. Wallace sees the adoption of an innovation as a two-step process. In the first step, the innovation must pass through a "psychological screen" that is used to reject innovations which are not compatible with the general society. The second step involves tests of acceptability by individual members of the society.

The psychological screen is seen as a filter imposed between the change agent and the society. The innovation must pass through this screen before it can be tried by the individuals in the society. What normally happens is that the leaders of the society evaluate the innovation to see if it is compatible with some structure of motives common in the society. If the leaders feel that the innovation is not compatible with the society's culture, they will reject it. Rejection by the leaders does not preclude subsequent use by members of the society. However, the growth in use of the innovation is severely retarded if the leaders do not back it.

It would seem that this is one reason why the backing of top management is so important for implementation of innovation. Members of top management are the leaders of the society (organization), and their backing of an idea is generally interpreted to mean that they have accepted it as being good for the people in the organization.

Acceptance by the leaders of the society does not necessarily mean that the innovation will be accepted by the individual members. The second part of the process is the individual test of acceptability. For this test, the criterion is the conviction that the innovation will contribute more to the satisfaction of a system of wants and needs than to their frustration. This is similar to the cost/benefit analysis, but it stresses the point that all innovations have both costs and benefits because they satisfy some needs while simultaneously frustrating others.

Wallace cautions that the change agent often overlooks the frustrating quality of an innovation as he stresses the benefits. He notes that there are many instances where the recipients of an innovation refused to accept it while the change agents expected them to embrace it warmly. According to Wallace (1970, p. 113), this is because

> The error of the donor generally lies in neglecting to assess the relevant negative functions of the proposed innovation; that is, in incorrectly identifying the institutionalized motives that the innovation would actually tend to frustrate.

Step two of the Wallace model thus reinforces the idea that the project manager must attempt to see the perception of the change from others' point of view. This means that he must understand as best he can both the positive and the negative aspects of the change from their point of view. For example, the project manager may see only the positive benefits of a change in accounting procedure as suggested in Chapter 6. With this in mind, he may go to the accounting department and propose the change. He may then be surprised when he is rebuffed by that department. It could be that his idea frustrates some need or desire on the part of the accounting department to keep all account codes uniform.

Given this example, the reader may well ask if awareness of others' frustration will help to change anything. Suppose the project manager is well aware of the accounting department's perceptions, but its members still will not change. Then what? To answer this, we will first consider the problems of being a change agent and then review the politics of implementation of change.

PATTERNS OF SUCCESSFUL CHANGE AGENTS

Donald Schon (1963) discovered a pattern of successful implementation from his study of champions for radical new inventions. He states that it is the nature of large organizations to oppose upsetting change and innovation. Top managers often have very thick screens which allow very few innovations to pass through for evaluation. Despite these thick screens, innovation does take place in both government and industry. The study of the history of these innovations is not a study of logic in decision making. It seems the histories look more like crusades or military campaigns, with overtones of fifth-column activity and guerrilla warfare. The histories do, however, provide clear illustrations of four major themes.

1. At the outset, the idea encounters sharp resistance.

Most new ideas run counter to established procedures. Few people immediately see the benefit of the new idea over the old procedure. The new way may be perceived as expensive and/or infeasible. So the idea is met with either indifference or active resistance.

2. Next, the idea receives active and vigorous promotion.

A vigorous internal sales campaign is necessary to overcome the initial resistance.

3. For the introduction, promotion, and development of these ideas, their proponents make use of the informal system.

Promotion of new ideas normally proceeds through the use of informal contacts within the organization. Often times funds are "detoured" from official programs to support initial experimentation with the idea. As an example, Arthur K. Watson has testified to the importance of this condition at IBM. He has stated:

> The disk memory unit, the heart of today's random access computer, is not the logical outcome of a decision made by IBM management. It was developed in one of our laboratories as a bootleg project—over the stern warning from management that the project had to be dropped because of budget difficulties. A handful of men ignored the warning. They broke the rules. They risked their jobs to work on a project they believed in. (quoted in Schon [1963])

4. Typically, one man emerges as champion of the idea.

Given the typical organizational resistance to innovation, any new idea either finds a champion or *dies*. The champion must be a person willing to put himself on the line for an idea of doubtful success. The person must be willing to fail but at the same time be ready to use any and every means of informal sales and pressure in order to succeed.

From this review and example, it would seem that few innovations are implemented based on their intrinsic merit alone. Those that are, such as the xerography machine, are those that immediately satisfy a universal need while frustrating very few. Such innovations are rare indeed. The more common pattern seems to be the need for a champion who is willing to put himself, and possibly his job, on the line in order to see an idea succeed. This person must be willing to use the informal network in the organization and to engage in the politics of the organization in order to make the idea succeed. However, because he will encounter the needs and values of others in the organization, even the best idea will be changed to some extent by the political process. Such is the life of the successful change agent.

THE POLITICS OF IMPLEMENTATION

Before beginning to engage in the political process, it is especially important to honestly consider the private language version of your values in relation to the changes you desire to implement. Other actors around you will see through your public language. If they do not find the outcome you desire to be congruent with their personal values, your public language will not ring true to them. They will look very carefully for private language interpretations of what you want. "The best strategy for the company" will quickly be seen by others as simply best to advance your career or nothing more than your personal preference. Even when others may agree with the outcome you prefer, they will still be aware of the private language interpretation as well as the public language interpretation. They will know what is in it for you. Thus it is important to be able to view your preferred outcomes from the point of view of others to see how they will react. In fully considering the private language, you will also better understand the full range of your own motivations.

After considering your own motivations, you should next scan the political field that surrounds you. Classifying the political forces at play will help to do this. Power can be classified into three types, from the strongest to the weakest. These types of power have been labeled control, influence, and appreciation by W. Smith (1983).

The strongest form of power is control. If you have control of an outcome, you are the only producer of that outcome. You do not rely on any other actor in the field. When this is the case, the probability of your producing the outcome that you desire is highest because you do not have to contend with the values and preferences of others. You depend solely on yourself.

Influence is not as strong as control. You have influence when you are the coproducer of an outcome, that is, when you and other actors produce the outcome together. One actor, alone, cannot do it by himself. The probability of success is lower than with control because you must rely on other actors, as well as yourself, to produce the outcome that you desire. Since other actors have their own desires, they may push the outcome in a direction that is different from the direction you want.

The weakest form of power is appreciation. When you have neither control nor influence over an outcome, you can only appreciate it. The outcome will be produced by other actors in the field, and their values will determine the direction and the nature of the outcome. You have no role in producing the outcome. Appreciation is a form of power because the alternative to appreciation is ignorance. If you can appreciate what lies behind those outcomes over which you have neither influence nor control, you can at least react to them so that they do not interfere with outcomes over which you do have control or influence. As your appreciation grows, you may even be able to devise methods to gain some influence over the outcome.

To ignore those outcomes which you cannot control or influence, or simply to accept them passively, is to remain powerless. For example, if I ignore or accept the rain, I will get wet. If I learn to appreciate it, I can use an umbrella and stay dry.

Individual managers deal primarily with influence and appreciation. Because to manage is to produce outcomes through others, we very rarely have complete control in managerial situations. Most of the time, the manager can only exert influence. This is because he is a coproducer of the outcome of the project along with the people that he manages. Unfortunately, there are also many aspects of a project which the manager cannot influence, only appreciate. These are the outcomes produced in other parts of the organization and in the environment of the organization to which project managers must react as they attempt to manage the project to completion.

This classification of power can be used at the group level as well as the individual level. As an individual manager, you do not really control the project that you head, even though you probably think of yourself as in control or out of control, depending on how the project is going. As a project manager, your influence on the outcome of the project can be very strong. The strength of the influence varies depending on how well you (or others) planned the project and how well you designed it to serve the values of the other actors who are the coproducers of the outcome.

If you think of the project team as an organizational actor, then it too controls, influences, and appreciates outcomes. Those outcomes which depend solely on members of the team (i.e., depend on actors fully contained within the boundaries of the project) are under the control of the project—not under your personal control, but under the project's control. Those outcomes which rely on other actors outside of the project team, as well as those within the team, are influenced by the project. Finally, those outcomes that depend solely on actors outside of the system can only be appreciated by the project team. Other actors may be individuals, groups, departments, other organizations, social forces, etc.

This method for viewing the political field becomes most useful in assessing the potential power of a project, anticipating problems, and then building a strategy and modifying that strategy as problems arise. The first two uses will be discussed next. The third use, building and modifying strategy, will then be considered in light of an added factor—the existence of multiple realities in any political system.

To assess how powerful a project is, simply assess the percentage of important outcomes that are under the project's control. Projects that are powerful (i.e., have the greatest probability of successful completion) are those in which the crucial outcomes are under the control of the project (at the group level). Sole production of those outcomes lies within the boundaries of the project itself. The power of the project weakens as more and more outcomes also depend on actors who are not contained within the boundaries of the project. When crucial outcomes depend solely on actors outside the boundaries of the project, the power of the project is severely weakened. The project team will be forced to react to the outcomes produced by others more than it will be able to act to produce its own outcomes. Many projects are designed so the project team's power is lower rather than higher. Critical outcomes are rarely under the control of the project; they are either influenced or appreciated. This is what makes project management more "political" than other types of management.

One can anticipate different kinds of problems based on the kinds of power at play in the project system, at the boundaries of the project, and in the wider environment of the project. In monitoring the progress of the project, make sure that those outcomes that are produced solely within the boundaries of the project are supported by a common "project culture," a shared vision of the desired outcomes, and a shared understanding of, and agreement on, responsibilities. However, circumstances can weaken a group's shared vision and understanding. These may slip from the group level into the individual level. For example, during a particularly tough time in the life of a project, a team member may begin to doubt the usefulness of the project. He begins to lose the vision and, therefore, his confidence that he will benefit from successful completion. His work begins to slip as he looks out for himself and prepares for failure instead of working for success. Others may be experiencing the same doubts, but no one talks about it for fear of being the only one. Thus the team members stop acting like a team and experiencing their "groupness." They act like a collection of individuals out for themselves at the expense of others on the team, and the project falls apart. Continuing use of team meetings to discuss progress, problems, and doubts can help to prevent this.

Those outcomes that depend on the project team and on other actors outside the project—those that are under the influence rather than the control of the project—bear more attention. They must be negotiated and renegotiated to completion. It is here that you can anticipate having a primary problem in "multiple realities." Those who are outside the project do not share the culture and the vision of the project. Because of this, they are more likely not only to be seeking different outcomes, but to be experiencing a different reality. Negotiation not only will involve coming to an agreement on the issues but may also involve creating a shared reality within which both parties can communicate and solve problems.

Finally, those outcomes which can only be appreciated by the project manager must be under constant surveillance. They will probably be the source of the most unpleasant surprises. This is the area in which good intelligence through the grapevine is essential, as is the ability to truly appreciate the underlying motives and values of the producing actors. Appreciate and anticipate so that you can react to produce and preserve the desired outcomes of the project.

Remember the problem with the accounting department mentioned earlier? One solution could be to explore the situation and negotiate with the accountant until you can find a modified accounting system that will meet your needs without violating his values. This means that you will probably have to modify your original idea to serve your own interests. For example, a two-part coding scheme may be agreed upon, the first part being your code and the second part being his. The important thing to remember is that your interests are to get a better accounting system to fit your needs, not to get your original idea rammed down the accountant's throat.

Building a strategy depends on an initial understanding of the political field that surrounds you as you plan, design, and begin to implement the project. It also depends on your ability to be flexible, to recognize the values of others, and to accept something different from what you thought you wanted when the project began. The real art of politics is to both get what you want and learn to want what you get. It is much easier to do this once you accept the fact that organizational life is full of multiple realities. Others in the organization experience reality differently from you. The project will not work unless it becomes acceptable in terms of a number of realities that may be very different from yours. This often means that the most successful project manager is the one who is ready to modify the perfect idea to fit political reality. He understands that a less than perfect idea that becomes reality is to be preferred over the perfect idea that is never implemented.

Understanding Multiple Realities

The essential principle which governs politics is the fact that social situations are characterized by the multiple realities of the participants in that situation (K. Smith, 1982). Conflicts and different desired outcomes arise not only because actors have different values but more often because actors experience a different reality even though they share the same situation. Take the example of two actors in the process of negotiation. The first actor, a manager who is in a position of authority in relation to the second, knows that he can get his way simply by "pulling rank." However, because he feels that the second manager has a good idea, he makes some concessions and feels that he has been very fair and has even done a favor for the second manager. The second manager knows that his own suggestion is the best way to proceed and is very frustrated that he is being blocked by the first manager in his position of authority. He experiences the concessions as token compromises given by a paternalistic, arrogant authority figure. Both managers leave the negotiation puzzled and frustrated because they were unable to experience each other's reality.

These multiple realities come from numerous sources in organizational life and have important consequences. Hierarchy is one primary source. Different functional positions, professional backgrounds, ethnic backgrounds, and sex roles, as well as other positional and role differences, represent other sources. Each instance creates a subculture in the organization through which actors interpret the world, evaluate it, and make choices to produce outcomes which they favor. This means that in all aspects of social life, different individuals and groups experience different realities even when they are in a common social space engaging in a collective action. Whether or not there is one true, objective, reality is irrelevant. People's interpretation of reality is what determines behavior. If two people interpret an event differently, their respective responses to that event will be different, and this will affect their behavior. Multiple realities are real in their consequences. Effective political strategies must be developed with this in mind.

Another example will help to further illustrate the power of multiple realities in human behavior. There is a simulation used in management development sessions to illustrate problems of competition and cooperation. It also illustrates multiple realities as well. The name of the game is "Win as Much as You Can," and the object of the game is to, of course, win as much as you can (Jones and Pfeiffer, 1975, pp. 62–67). Participants are placed in teams of two, and four teams are put into a cluster. The game is a collective version of the prisoner's dilemma. In a series of rounds, each team must decide whether to hold up a Y or an X to receive a payoff. The payoff is determined by what letter the other three teams in the cluster choose as well. If every team in a cluster holds up a Y, each team wins one point. If every team holds up an X each team loses one point. However, when some teams hold up X's while others hold up Y's, teams with X's win points while those with Y's lose points. A "win-win" strategy of everyone choosing Y's will maximize points for the whole cluster, but a "win-lose" strategy of voting an X while other teams vote Y will maximize a team's points. For the first four rounds, there is no communication between teams in a cluster. For the fifth, eighth, and tenth rounds, teams within a cluster may communicate with each other before the vote.

The basic driving principle of the game is governed by how each participant interprets the word "you" in the phrase "win as much as *you* can" and how that interpretation frames the reality that is experienced during the course of the game. There are four possibilities for interpreting the word "you." The most obvious and usually the first to enter participants' experience is that "you" refers to the team within a cluster. Based on this interpretation, each team begins to develop a strategy to maximize its payoffs in relation to the other teams in the cluster.

As the game progresses through the first few rounds, teams begin to realize that they are often blocked from their objective by the actions of other teams in their cluster. Some begin to consider another interpretation of the word "you." "You" may also refer to the cluster in relation to the other clusters in the room. Another set of behaviors based on negotiations during rounds five, eight, and ten can maximize the payoffs for the cluster as a whole—all four teams in the cluster voting Y. Some teams may realize this and attempt to bring the other teams in their cluster to this interpretation, to enter this new reality. Only if all the teams in the cluster accept the new reality and act on it will the cluster experience it.

It is most interesting to observe this game in progress because the political process of multiple realities and their behavioral consequences surfaces so dramatically. In a recent session, there were three clusters. In the first cluster, there developed a very strong sense of frustration. Most of the teams had realized that the cluster interpretation of the word "you" was possible and would jointly optimize their collective payoffs, but they could not trust each other enough to change their behavior. In each round, one or another team would bolt the "new order" and vote with an X to maximize the team payoff instead of with a Y to jointly optimize the cluster's payoff. When this happened, the other teams in the cluster received negative payoffs. No one team consistently deviated, rather they almost took turns. This led to the growing sense of frustration that they could not create in behavioral terms what they could envision in their minds and even talk about during the negotiation rounds.

The quality in the second cluster was very different. Here, one group led by a financial analyst locked into the team level of reality as the absolutely correct and final truth. This was obviously (to them) a game of mathematical maximization for each team. To maximize winnings (or minimize losings) a team merely had to always vote with an X. This one team was impervious to any arguments, negotiations, or form of persuasion and/or coercion exerted by other teams in the cluster as these other teams began to attempt to actualize their new version of collective reality for the cluster. While the first cluster was characterized by a sense of frustration, this cluster exhibited raw anger. The resistant team was subjected to verbal abuse and ostracized by the end of the game. Its members were still trying to justify their behavior well after the game had ended and were constantly the subject of jokes by members of their cluster for the rest of the day.

The third cluster was able to actualize the more collective interpretation of "you" very quickly. These teams all hit upon it during the first two rounds, experienced it before they even went into a negotiation round, and worked very hard to maintain it throughout the rest of the game. There were a few instances of "deviant" behavior, but the group was able to bring doubting teams back into the collective reality during subsequent negotiation rounds.

The differences among these clusters became immediately obvious through observing their behavior. The first cluster quickly became lackadaisical. Negotiation sessions were held by talking from sitting positions without much energy or expectation. Teams became more intense after the cluster negotiation, talking only to themselves during the period of decision before they were to vote.

The second cluster was more intense during cluster negotiations. Most of the energy was focused on the one team that refused to change its behavior. Everyone was faced in the direction of that team, but no one moved towards it. Near the end of the rounds, most people in the second cluster were sitting in their seats with their arms folded, which symbolizes a very defensive posture.

The third cluster literally jumped into the cluster negotiation sessions. Everyone got out of their chairs and huddled. Primary energy was focused on the cluster meetings. When teams were asked to decide their vote after a cluster meeting, they hardly talked, as if their vote had already been decided in the previous cluster meeting. Not only had members of the third group been able to think about a different interpretation of reality, they were able to actualize it and, therefore, experience it. Once they had collectively framed a new reality, they were able to share it, act on it, and experience it. The other two clusters continued to be blocked and frustrated, by the multiple realities within the group.

A project team is much like one of these clusters. Team members need to share a common interpretation of organizational life in relation to the project and to share a common set of values to produce project outcomes. Tactics within the project system should work to keep the subculture intact so that each member develops a common vision and understanding. Design, planning meetings, memos, conversations, and all other forms of communication to begin a project build an important foundation. When team members begin the project with a collective image and a common set of values, this increases the probability that they will begin acting like a team from the very beginning. When they actually experience themselves as a team, the experience will reinforce the image and values.

Participative planning and other tools such as responsibility charting are important to help define the collective image. However, doing this kind of work merely at the beginning of the project is usually not enough to ensure that the image continues through project execution. Similar work throughout the course of the project is essential to maintain the synergy of the project team.

Individual project members can easily slip back into individual interpretations of collective events. Because of this, they may begin to lose some trust in one another and in the project manager. One way to prevent this is to expect it and encourage team members to talk about negative experiences, as well as positive ones, with each other and in periodic review sessions.

These meetings need to be characterized by an atmosphere in which members are free to vent frustrations and even suspicions that others are not working in the collective interest. This is a very important way to open each member of the team to the reality experienced by others on the team. From this openness, the group will begin to further enrich the common aspects of the reality its members experience as a team. Team members should also be able to express their feelings about events and actions of others. The idea is to keep the group in touch with the collective values, while honestly acknowledging that certain aspects of experience may run counter to these values and then working as a team to minimize the risk of countering experience to the values of the group. By doing this, the project team will maintain its collective control over outcomes within the project boundary. Its members will also be better able to influence those outcomes which span the boundary of the project team because they will be negotiating from a common understanding of what they want.

Negotiating outside the Team

As the project unfolds and proceeds, there will be a constant need for all project members to negotiate with individuals and groups outside the project team. This is because many of the outcomes desired by the project team members depend on others outside the project team as well. There are a number of excellent books on negotiation which should be part of every manager's tool kit (e.g., Fischer and Ury, 1981; Raiffa, 1982).

There are two major principles that need to be remembered while negotiating. The first is the principle of multiple realities, which has been discussed. The second is the associated problem of project team members' engaging with the realities of other groups in order to negotiate with them, yet still maintaining their participation in the reality of the project team itself (Miller and Rice, 1975, pp. 59-62).

In negotiating with systems outside the project team, members of the project will have to see reality in terms of other actors in order to engage with them and arrive at acceptable solutions to problems that are encountered. This will probably involve changing some assumptions and interpretations of reality originally shared with members of the project team. Thus, the successful act of negotiation actually "pollutes" those members of the team who engage in the negotiations. They may come back to the project team with solutions that are seen by the rest of the team as a "sellout." This begins to erode the synergy of the team, and before anyone realizes what is happening, things begin to fall apart internally.

There is no sure way to prevent this, but being aware of the possibility is the beginning of prevention. The role given to a negotiator should be made very clear by the project team. Negotiators are sent out from a group with one of three possible roles. First, they may be emissaries with no real negotiating power at all; their role is simply to listen, observe, and report back to the team. Second, they may represent the team. In this role, the negotiator can engage in the negotiation process but cannot enter into a final decision without getting approval from the team. The third role is that of autonomous negotiator. In this role, the negotiator has full authority to enter into final decisions without checking back with the team.

In the first role, the team will not be threatened, but no negotiations will take place. The second role provides a check on the negotiator to keep him from being influenced too much by the needs and reality of other actors outside the team, but it also reduces his power and flexibility in the negotiations. The third role requires the highest level of trust by the project team in the negotiator, and gives him the highest degree of flexibility and power to negotiate with the other party. It requires that team members feel that the negotiator did negotiate the best deal under the circumstances and that he fully represented the interests of the team during the negotiations. In both the second and the third roles, negotiators will have to come back to the team and show how the negotiated solution really does fit the collective image and values held by the team.

Whatever the negotiated settlement, it will be different from an idealized solution created without regard to outside actors in the field. This means that the project teams should process the events that the team influences. This should be done in the same way as they process events that are under the team's control.

Finally, the project team should constantly engage in a collective process of appreciating those outcomes which lie outside the project boundaries and are neither controlled nor influenced by the project team. As the project proceeds, new events which can only be appreciated will take place. The team should incorporate the experience of these events into its collective consciousness through discussion and strategy sessions. This will enable the project team to better coordinate its response to the unexpected and/or to anticipate developing outcomes and better coordinate its response to the expected. As these events unfold, the group may be able, through the collective appreciation process, to develop strategies to bring some of these outcomes under the influence of the project.

There are no simple recipes to solve the problems associated with the politics of implementation. There are, however, important principles to keep in mind while engaging in the implementation process. Once the project begins, you are no longer dealing with images alone. You are now dealing with experience. As people experience the action of others, this will influence the images they hold. It will influence

their values and their reality. Experience should be processed as it unfolds. It should be a topic of discussion at emotional levels as well as cognitive levels. "How did you feel?" should be as legitimate a question as "What do you think?" Multiple realities must be acknowledged. They are the prime cause of conflict. They will not go away if ignored but rather will become more powerful in preventing individuals and groups from getting what they want. When multiple realities are surfaced and shared, they become the basis for developing a shared reality to build a team, negotiate with others, and better appreciate those outcomes controlled by forces outside the spheres of your influence and control. Working with multiple realities is the essential element of exercising your power—control, influence, and appreciation.

Finally, when all is said and done, it is the ability to stick to it, to not give up in the face of overwhelming odds and impossible resistance, that will spell the difference between success and failure. One builds a strategy for project implementation because he knows any kind of organizational change takes a long time. Strategies are useful because they are broad and flexible. It is a matter not of "*Will* I change my strategy over the life of a project?" but rather of "*How will* I change it?" The successful project manager learns to fit his preferred outcomes with the preferences of other actors around him, and in doing so he necessarily modifies his preferences. The politics of implementation is the process of learning to collaborate with the political forces that surround you in the organization.

AN IMPLEMENTATION PLAN

By this point, it should be clear that implementation of change is a process rather than an event. The following 12 steps to implementing change are based on the discussions contained both in this and in other chapters:

1. *Decide that you really want to do it.* It would seem that very little change will take place without your absolute commitment. As far as change is concerned, the bureaucracy should be seen as a hindrance and not a help. The project manager must be the champion for the changes that he or she deems necessary.

2. *Decide what you really want to do.* Here the project manager specifies the behavior that he is going to exhibit and the behavior that is desired from others.

3. *Consider others' values and multiple realities.* Remember that your solution is someone else's problem. Consider *your* solution in the light of *his* reality. List the values that will be served by your proposed changes, and list the values that will be frustrated. For those whose values will be served, devise a plan to inform them of all the benefits of your proposed changes. For those whose values will be frustrated, determine your power in the situation. If you have direct control, you may not be too concerned. If you have only influence, you may want to use informal sources, particularly those whose values will be served, in order to maximize your influence. If you can only appreciate, you may want to consider giving up the scheme or create a longer-term strategy to develop influence from appreciation.

4. *Obtain top management support.* Remember that this is the most important variable for success in most studies of successful implementation.

5. *Publicize your plan with information.* This is the second most important variable for successful implementation. Tell everyone what it is you want to do, why you want to do it from your standpoint, and what is in it for them if they change their behavior.

6. *Stress the vision.* Continue to stress the end point, what you think life will be like in the future. The vision must be communicated repeatedly because many people have trouble comprehending what they have not experienced. There will be initial doubt and resistance, but remember that belief begins with doubt.

7. *Teach the new behavior.* People are often asked to engage in behavior which they do not know how to perform. A simple example is asking someone to do a PERT chart who does not have the necessary background knowledge. Be certain that people have the knowledge and skills necessary to perform the new behavior.

8. *Exhibit the new behavior.* This is teaching by role model, probably the most effective method known. It is usually fruitless to

ask someone else to engage in behavior that you do not engage in yourself. This gives a signal that you do not really believe in it. When you role-model behavior, you indicate your commitment.

9. *Reward the new behavior.* It is a well-known folly to ask for behavior A while rewarding behavior B. Many people forget that rewards send a powerful signal concerning what is valued in an organization. The rewards do not necessarily have to be money, but they should be something that the receiver values.

10. *Take time.* Thought patterns are deeply ingrained and take much time to change. Asking for radical change in a short period of time could frustrate people's values unnecessarily. An important ingredient in any change program is simply allowing enough time.

11. *Keep at it.* Remember that while it will take more time than you would like, you will still have to continuously push the project to completion. Change will not take place if you simply suggest it and then wait for it to happen.

12. *Be prepared to get what you want and learn to want what you get.* Success is not necessarily getting the outcome that you thought you wanted at the beginning of the project. As you become more sensitive to the values and realities of others, you will probably change your preferred outcomes. Remember that success is a completed project, not the perfect idea that never becomes part of the organizational experience.

SUMMARY

The complete project manager sees himself as a change agent. As such, the complete project manager understands the politics of the organization of which the project is a part and considers political maneuvering as a part of the job. As much as possible, the complete project manager shields the project team from outside influence. The complete project manager understands those aspects of the project's destiny over which he has control, those where he can influence and those where he can only appreciate. By accepting the role of change agent, the complete project manager devises a plan for change and understands the precariousness of the role. The complete project manager and change agent takes Machiavelli's quote (at the beginning of this chapter) to heart.

REFERENCES

Dane, C. W., Gray, C. F., and Woodworth, B. "Successfully Introducing Project Management Techniques into an Organization," *Project Management Quarterly,* December 1981.

Davis, E. W. "Networks: Resource Allocation," *Industrial Engineering,* April 1974.

Fischer, R. and Ury, W. *Getting to Yes: Negotiating Agreement without Giving In.* Boston: Houghton Mifflin, 1981.

Jones, J. E. and Pfeiffer, J. W. *A Handbook of Structured Experiences for Human Relations Training,* Vol. II. La Jolla: University Associates, 1975.

Lorsch, J. W. *Managing Change,* ICCH Case No. 9-474-187. Boston: Harvard Business School, 1974.

Miller, E. J. and Rice, A. K. "Selections from Systems of Organization," in *Group Relations Reader.* (A. D. Colman and W. H. Bexton, Eds.). Sausalito: GREX, 1975.

Raiffa, H. *The Art and Science of Negotiation.* Boston: Harvard University Press, 1982.

Schon, D. A. "Champions for Radical New Inventions," *Harvard Business Review,* 1963.

Smith, K. *Groups in Conflict.* Dubuque: Kendall/Hunt, 1982.

Smith, W. "Organizing as a Power Process: The Creation and Testing of a Conceptual Framework and Its Application to the Design of Development Projects." Ph.D. Dissertation, Social Systems Sciences Department, The Wharton School, 1983.

Urban, G. L. "Building Models for Decision Makers," *Interfaces,* 1974, **4,** 1-11.

Wallace, A. F. C., *Culture and Personality* (2nd. Edition) New York: Random House, 1970.

Youker, R. "Implementing Change in Organizations (a Manager's Guide)," *Project Management Quarterly,* March 1983.

Index

Index